HORRIFIC ENDEAVORS

Horrific Endeavors

KATO M. M. GUZMAN

CONTENTS

Horrific Endeavors

Copyright © 2024 by Kato M. M. Guzman

Published by Kato M. M. Guzman & Slingstone Media

No part of this book may be reproduced, distributed, or transmitted in any form or by any means, including photocopying, recording, or other electronic or mechanical methods, without the prior written permission of the author, except in the case of brief quotations embodied in critical reviews and certain other noncommercial uses permitted by copyright law.

This is a work of fiction. Names, characters, businesses, places, events, and incidents are either the product of the author's imagination or used in a fictitious manner. Any resemblance to actual persons, living or dead, or actual events is purely coincidental.

Ebook ISBN: 979-8-3306-3094-3

ISBN: 979-8-3304-9877-2

Cover Design: Kato M. M. Guzman

First Edition: 2024

For permissions requests:

Katommguzman.com

For Karl, one of my oldest friends and earliest
supporters.
You believed in me as a writer long before I did.
We miss you, brother.

Introduction

After years of sending submissions to publishers with no interest in signing a new writer like me, I decided it was time to tell these tales without permission. Observers have noted that a majority of writers, including newly signed writers, are white. I'm not blaming my failures on my ethnicity, or looking to accuse anyone of anything. It's hard to look past the data and know whether I failed to make it in the industry on the fault of my writing, or if there were deep-rooted systemic biases running against me. It's an easy excuse to have, it alleviates me of responsibility, but there's a reason this thought wormed its way into my brain.

The real wake-up call came while workshopping a story in a horror writers' group. I shared a piece called *Tao-taomona Woman*, deeply inspired by my family and Chamorro heritage.

The feedback I received missed the essence of the story. They wanted a more monstrous taotaomona, more horror, less culture. But the taotaomona—a spirit central to Chamorro beliefs—wasn't some random monster. Symbolizing my cultural roots and the complex ways we, as diasporic islanders, try to belong to traditions that are both ours and elusive, it represented a lot. It wasn't about the taotaomona haunting; it was about my haunting distance from my culture, the bittersweet way our heritage can both bind us and slip through our fingers.

I made the edits they wanted, focusing more on terror than cultural meaning, and felt the soul of the story slip away. The story that remained wasn't the one I intended to tell. There are calls from across the literary world for more work from persons of color and indigenous writers like myself and yet, we're often dismissed or misunderstood. The data tells us that our chances are far fewer than the same odds for a person with a "normal" sounding name.

I did what people like me have done more and more over the years: turned to self publishing. If I'm going to fail or succeed, it will be on my own terms and it won't be without a fight. Taotaomona Woman appears in this collection as I intended it from the start. I took their notes into consideration for improvement, where they fit without costing the soul of the story.

Horrific Endeavors is a collection I'm putting out myself. It's a DIY project built from years of skill-building as a multimedia journalist, filmmaker, and writer. I wrote every story, designed the artwork, handled the layout, and pulled this collection together with a commitment to authenticity using the best tools at my fingertips. We're all alone in this world, and all we have are the thoughts that haunt us. The only difference between myself and a madman is that I wrote my thoughts on these pages and sent it out into the world to sow chaos and disorder.

Because I'm talking about race, ignorance and deep-rooted racism, doesn't mean this is another story made for persons of color, or an inspirational collection of wonderful pieces of literature that generations to follow will point to as a guiding light. I'm nobody's savior or spokesperson. I speak only for myself and the voices in my head.

This is horror, plain and simple—no trigger warnings, no holds barred. Blood, gore, killers, spirits, sorrow, joy, tragedy—it's all here. The darkness in this book speaks for itself. There's magic and evil in all forms. It has heart as much as it has heartlessness. It has beauty and tragedy, elation and depravity.

There are evil things in this world, and it is my deepest hope that this book becomes one of those evil things. I want to fuel your nightmares to steal every ounce of sleep I can steal.

Good luck and enjoy the horrific endeavors captured within these pages.

| 1 |

JESTER

The jester, charged with insulting the king and his heirs, took his place beneath the guillotine and looked to the executioner. "A little off the top, please," he said, moments before his head rolled across the stage.

| 2 |

SLASHERS SLASHING SLASHERS: THE LAST REST STOP

Easton took a drag off his joint. The faces of everyone they killed and everything they did to them flooded his mind. He exhaled a plume of smoke and felt a wave of calm wash over him as the truck bobbed along on the road. The memories faded and his mind returned to the present. He laid on the bed in the camper. Beneath him, in the truck cabin below, Wes drove and Britney sat shotgun.

Her hand hung out the window, gliding up and down, riding the waves of the balmy summer wind. Her rings and bracelets shimmered in the last bit of sun as it descended below the mountains. Cascading tendrils of her blonde hair swayed in the truck's wake as it sped down the highway.

To divert her thoughts from her father's imminent execution, which had endured four harrowing postponements, Britney sought solace in the wind's embrace. Her father, once dubbed The Unkillable Killer by the headlines, had finally met his match, and his life would draw to a close by week's end.

Wes sang along to an embarrassing pop song in the driver's seat. He screamed at an obnoxious volume, as off pitch as he could get, a playful mockery masking his familiarity with the song's every word. His hulking frame appeared small in the spacious confines of his new truck, a gift from his father for getting into an Ivy League. Possessing the rugged jawline of a high school athlete, his eyes held a hint of sensitive introspection akin to a poet, yet his true demeanor was more akin to bratty entitled youth.

Britney pulled Wes's varsity jacket close over her shoulders and rolled up the window. The day grew old, and the night grew cold. No more surfing hands.

The song faded, and at an interlude in the music, Easton knocked. She turned down the music as the next song started and slid open the window between the truck and the camper.

"We're almost there," Tracy said, pushing Easton aside.

Tracy's big brown eyes gazed through the window, surrounded by heavy eye shadow and thick lashes. Her septum piercing shimmered as the headlights of the truck switched on.

"Alright," Wes said. "We'll keep an eye out."

Tracy, Chris and Easton stowed away in the truck bed camper. The camper had a bathroom/shower, though none of them ever wanted to use it, so instead it became an impromptu storage. There was a small stove and a fridge, which held enough food and drinks for small stretches of their journey. A bench wrapped around a table that transformed into a bed. A large window, covered by a thick blackout curtain, ran alongside.

Easton sprawled out in the bed above at the front of the camper, blowing smoke out from the overhead emergency escape hatch. The aroma wafted down into the cab. Britney cracked her window back open to get fresh air.

"Who sings that song you were just playing?" Easton asked, pushing Tracy aside.

"Olivia Rodrigo, why?" Britney answered.

"Yeah, let's keep it that way, Wes. Thanks," Easton said.

"Asshole," Wes said.

Wes let out a small laugh, but Britney knew it stung. They drove in silence after that, mentally preparing. Up ahead, thick woods, nestled in the crevice of two mountains, ate the road. As they neared, Britney adjusted in her seat.

"You okay?" Wes asked.

"I'm good. After all this open road, it feels a little…"

"Claustrophobic?"

"I guess. You can see trouble coming a mile away when there's nothing around. In the woods, you can't see any-thing."

They made their way deeper into the woods and up the mountain. Darkness took hold and stars rose in the sky, only visible through occasional cracks in the branches. They made their way through the winding roads, peering out the window.

"Guys, I think I see someone up ahead," Wes called back.

A tiny figure caught the light of the truck.

"Hitchhiker," Chris said.

A lone figure paced along the side of the road. Walking backwards, he held his right arm out with a straight thumb pointing upwards. He waved big and wide with his other arm and had a large smile plastered across his face, surrounded by thick stubble and a mop of hair. Across his forehead, he wore a dirty red bandana.

"This is how horror movies start," Britney said.

"Let's pick him up," Wes said.

Wes drove past the hitchhiker, but slowed, then pulled over down the road. The hitchhiker jogged up to the truck. Wes drove slow enough for the hitchhiker to keep pace as Britney leaned out the window.

She put on a show, acting the part everyone expected of her. Voice soft with childlike innocence, sentences ending like a question, eyes wide and a big smile plastered across her face. The beautiful, innocent blonde.

"Where are you headed?" Britney asked.

"Wherever the road takes me, gorgeous," the hitchhiker said.

"You've been walking for a while?" Britney looked back down the dark empty road behind.

"All day, I haven't seen many cars. If you can give me a lift, I'd really appreciate it. Anywhere. As far as you'll take me."

"Afraid there's not so much room up here with me and Wes, but my sister and her friends are in the camper, if you're okay riding back there with them?"

"Oh really? Yeah, that'd be great."

"Beer or water?"

"Beer sounds fantastic if you have one," he said.

"Great!"

Wes slowed the car to a stop, and the hitchhiker walked around back to the camper, where Tracy opened the door and held out a cold beer.

"Hey! I'm Tracy. Easton is the guy who smells like weed, and Chris is the guy who looks mad that Easton smells like weed. Come on in."

Tracy too played the part expected of her. It was always disarming when she put on the act. Where Britney played the clueless ditz, Tracy played the edgy alternative girl.

The hitchhiker grabbed the ladder next to the door and pulled himself up into the camper, accepting the beer and taking a swig as he made his way in. Easton sat on the bed and stared up at the ceiling, ignoring their new travel buddy. Chris stood beside the table and motioned for their guest to have a seat at the table. Tracy squeezed in across the table, leaning forward and letting him think she had an interest in dirty vagrants.

"Thanks," the stranger said.

He plopped his backpack against the wall beside him. Chris closed the camper door and sat beside Tracy. The truck jerked forward and rocked as Wes continued to drive. Britney and Wes stayed silent as they listened to their plan unfold with the stranger in the camper.

"You look tired," Chris said, taking a sip of water.

"Chris! That isn't a nice thing to say," Tracy said, mimicking Britney's own valley girl personality as part of her cover. "I'm sure you'd look tired too if you hiked through those woods. It looks so scary out there. Where'd you come from?"

She took a drink from her beer. He did the same. It was a tactic Easton taught them to lull targets into a false sense of security. Show interest, flatter them. When you steal their attention, you can trick them into drinking when you want them to drink, and what you want them to drink.

"Nowhere in particular," he said, looking from Chris to Tracy, back to Chris.

Easton laid on the bed, listening and not offering much to the conversation. He had a job to do. He had to count. So he counted and waited.

"Where are you from?" Chris asked. "You know, originally?"

"Bottoms up," Tracy said. She clinked her glass against the stranger's, then chugged her beer. The stranger did the same.

"From Colorado, but I haven't been there for a while. What about you? Where are you guys heading? Where are you guys from?"

"Well, I grew up around—" Tracy began. Easton shot up into a sitting position. Everyone looked at Easton. He nodded to Chris and pointed to his wrist as if showing a time.

Easton climbed down from the bed and sat next to their guest.

"Who's your favorite scream queen?" Easton asked.

"Scream queen? You mean like the final girl?"

"No, a final girl is the last girl to survive a horror movie. A scream queen is an actress who often does horror roles. My favorite is Emma Roberts. I loved her in *Scream 4*, *Blackcoat's Daughter*, and, of course, *Scream Queens*."

"He thinks she's hot," Tracy said, rolling her eyes. "My favorite is Jamie Lee Curtis. She's classic, yet modern, and she seems to just enjoy everything about life now. That's what I love about a scream queen. So who's yours?"

"I'm not really a horror fan," he said.

"It's okay, you don't have to be," Easton said.

"What's that one movie called? *I Spit on Your Grave.* That chick, I guess."

"A rape revenge movie? Seriously? Figures." Tracy said.

"Tracy..." Chris said, signaling for her not to say what he knew she was about to say, but he couldn't stop the inevitable. She broke character and let her true self shine.

"Keep *I Spit on Your Grave* and give me a sequel to *You're Next.* Rape revenge flicks are the epitome of exploitation. It's a blatant oversimplification of justice and a perpetuation of harmful stereotypes. Reducing a woman to a beaten down, broken mess while she screams and cries and her tits bounce around. Look at that movie, or at *Straw Dogs, Last House on the Left.* Hillbillies, rednecks, local idiots who don't know their dicks from their tits. You want a real rape revenge fantasy? Set it in a boardroom in a corporate office and have it called *The Last Office on the Left* or *I Spit on Your Stock Options.* Wes Craven would have done the concept justice. But then I guess there's *Blink Twice.*"

Easton nodded over to the hitchhiker for Tracy to look. The hitchhiker's eyelids drooped and his head bobbed like a toddler fighting a nap in the car.

"I guess your little speech put him to sleep," Easton said.

Chris looked into those droopy eyes.

"Are you sure you're from Colorado? Not Minnesota? Duluth?" Chris asked.

The hitchhiker glanced from Tracy to Chris. He fiddled with the bottle in his hand. Easton felt the camper shaking as the hitchhiker's leg bounced beneath the table.

"Duluth? Never been."

"You sure about that, Ken?" Tracy asked.

The stranger's eyes bulged.

"What'd you call me?"

He rubbed his eyes, trying to focus. His leg stopped bouncing.

"Ken? Or Kenneth?"

"How'd you know my name? I haven't—"

"So you are Kenneth from Duluth? Kenneth Anderson?"

"What is this? Who are you people?"

He tried to stand, but his eyes rolled to the back of his head. His eyelids grew heavy, and he did his best to look at Tracy and Chris from beneath them. Easton pushed his way through and stared into Kenneth's eyes.

"Damn, there must have been half a bottle in his beer. Guy must be tweaking," Easton said.

Kenneth's eyes shut as his body fell forward and slammed against the table. His arms fell limp to his side. The empty beer bottle slipped from his hand and onto the floor.

"Finally," Tracy said, back to her normal self. Her voice was deeper and filled with annoyance.

"Hey, this isn't easy," Easton said. "I didn't even know what he looked like in person, let alone what drugs he's already on or what he weighed."

"It's fine, Easton. You did good," Chris said. He leaned down to the window of the truck. "Okay, he's out cold."

"Where's the map?" Wes asked.

Chris pulled the map out from his back pocket. For things like this, he preferred old school paper maps. It's easy to mark up and doesn't leave a digital trail.

Chris opened the map and dragged his finger down their path. He dragged his finger further down the road to a small offshoot and a rest stop marker. He had a few notes scribbled there. Further on, he dragged his finger. He pursed his lips in thought.

"In about two miles, there's a road that goes nowhere, but it's not paved. There's also an abandoned rest stop in three miles that might be good."

"Which is it, Chris?" Wes shouted back.

"Rest stop, take the rest stop," Easton shouted over Chris' answer.

"Rest stop works for me," Chris said.

"You sure it's him?" Britney asked.

"It's him," Tracy shouted back. She waved something in the air but realized Britney couldn't see it, so she walked it over and handed it through the window. It was his wallet, his ID taken out and held on top.

"Kenneth Michael Anderson," Britney said. She put his ID behind his wallet and started going through it. "No cash. Memberships to businesses that closed in the 90s. Anything good back there?"

"Not yet," Tracy shouted back as she dumped the hitchhiker's backpack onto the table. She scattered his belongings around.

Chris stuck his fingers into a tiny pocket on the backpack inside the main flap and pulled something out. Tracy's eyes widened at the heart-shaped pendant dangling from a silver necklace.

"That looks familiar," Tracy said.

She shoved aside a few of Kenneth's belongings and set up a laptop. After clicking around, she showed Chris.

"Bingo," Chris said.

"What is it?" Britney asked.

He put the necklace to the side and continued digging through the small pockets. After a few moments of searching, he pulled out something else and held it up for Tracy. A few clicks at the keyboard and Tracy turned the laptop and once again showed Chris.

"Hello?" Britney said. "What is it?"

Tracy moved to the window of the cab and held out the laptop. On it was a picture of diamond earrings, a perfect match for the two Tracy held in her gloved hand. Britney smiled.

They spent some time sorting through everything on the table and in the backpack and returned whatever seemed irrelevant.

Tracy organized the necklace, the earrings, and a few other items they identified. She took each of those items and placed them into plastic bags, then labeled them with names of the people to whom they once belonged.

From a concealed compartment beneath the sink, Easton retrieved a duffel bag, unveiling their distinctive skull masks, each one's hollow gaze meeting his.

He handed one to Chris, who pulled it over his head and put his hood up. They customized each mask for their owner. Chris's mask bore a weathered, off-white visage with skillful black brushstrokes, mimicking the appearance of a genuine, aged skull.

Easton presented an intricately designed skull mask to Tracy, painted in the vibrant style of a sugar skull offered to the departed on Dia de los Muertos.

He slid Wes's through the window, and Britney handed it over. He laid his across his lap. The eyes made it hard to see the road, and they still had a short drive left.

Britney took her skull. It was a pastel pink, dry brushed and weathered with black. Across the lips was a thick smear of red lipstick. She wasn't happy with her mask at first, but she couldn't think of anything else. Art was never a strong hobby for her. The more they killed, the more she grew to love the mask despite the chic aesthetic.

Easton took the last mask and placed it on his head. His skull was black and dry brushed white, like the charred skull found in the aftermath of a fire. The eyes had an ominous sadness to them.

Britney knelt on the seat of the truck, watching Tracy organize their hostage's belongings. The truck came to a halt.

"Hey, guys? We have a problem," Wes said.

Easton looked through the window to the cab and saw the headlights illuminating a locked gate. It was a swing gate like what a farmer would use for trails where they herd livestock. Vegetation, weeds and grass, tiny stems of trees and poison ivy, grew across the paved road and up the gate, choking it.

"You didn't say anything about a gate," Wes said.

"I didn't know there was a gate," Easton said. "Most of the pictures and videos were older. They probably put it up to keep people out."

"Oh really? They put it up to keep people out? No shit, why else would they put up a gate?"

"Hey, man, I did my job fine. Is it locked? Just open it and go through," Easton said, rolling his eyes.

"Why don't you go check if it's locked?"

"Fine. It's not a big deal, dude."

Easton climbed out of the back of the camper, jumping down and kicking up a cloud of dirt. It settled like a creeping fog in the red taillights of the idling truck. The unexpected cold crept through Easton's thin t-shirt, making him shiver. Moonlight drifted through the branches, leaking only enough to let the trees look like reaching hands.

He made his way around the truck, cursing beneath his breath at the cold. Something icy touched his shoulder. A shiver shot down his spine. He spun around and saw the empty eyes of Britney's skull mask staring at him from the darkness, her hand on his shoulder.

"Scared? You gotta lay off the weed," Britney said. "I think there's a lock on the gate."

Easton nodded and shook his shoulders, as if loosening them and discarding his fear. She followed him over to the gate and sure enough, there was a chain wrapped with a thick padlock locking the gate to the pillar on the side.

Any other person might have stopped and found another place to go, but Easton embraced obstacles he could over-come with a video tutorial. In fact, months prior, he had perfected the breaking of padlocks and started teaching Britney the craft. He retrieved a trusted screwdriver, often used for fixing his problematic weed grinder.

"Want to try?" Easton asked.

"I'll let the master work," Britney said. "Consider it a teachable moment."

He jabbed the screwdriver into the keyhole and shook it around, sliding it back and forth. From his pocket, he retrieved another handy tool, the wonderful paperclip. With these tools at his disposal, nothing could stop him. He bent the paperclip and jammed it into the lock with the screwdriver and fiddled them around in the keyhole. A few minutes passed, and he stepped back, dropping the screwdriver and paperclip into his pocket.

Something brushed against the back of his neck, and a voice seemed to scream out from the darkness.

"What are you so—"

"Jesus Christ!" Easton screamed as jumped a foot in the air and stumbled into the hood of the truck.

Wes knelt down, took the lock in his hand and inspected it.

"Why would you do that?" Easton cried out.

"What are you so proud of? It's still locked," Wes said.

Easton walked up to the lock, still in Wes's hand and kicked it. Wes dropped the lock and jumped back as Easton's foot slammed into it, narrowly missing Wes's fingers.

"Why would you do that?" Wes yelled back at Easton.

Easton didn't say a thing. He turned and walked back to the camper. Wes looked over at the lock. It lay on the ground, the lock open, the chain dangling off the gate. He rolled his eyes and opened the creaky gate, then he and Britney hopped into the truck and made their way in.

"Easton," Wes called back through the window to the camper.

"What?"

"Fuck you, man."

The truck slowed as it circled the rest stop, making sure there was no one around. Chris pulled back the curtain inside the camper and looked out.

"This is creepier than I expected," he said. Easton leaned on his shoulder and looked outside.

"I mean, I expected it to be creepy," Easton said. "It's an abandoned rest stop. Don't know what you expected."

The rest stop was a small building with a women's restroom on one side and a men's restroom on the other. Graffiti covered the walls. The door to the men's room hung off the hinges. The tiny building looked small, surrounded by parking spots stretching out to the surrounding woods.

The truck pulled around the rear of the building and backed to the edge of the woods. Wes and Britney climbed out and stretched their arms to the sky like infants waking up from a long nap. Wes cracked his neck and popped his arms and squatted down, letting out more pops from his knees.

"That's so gross," Britney said.

"Those are the pops of an athletic body," Wes said.

"Yeah, a fifty-year-old athlete, you're 18."

"Are you guys ready?" Wes asked.

They each nodded and gave a verbal confirmation, part of their agreement. If any of them had any doubts, they expected for them to voice their concerns. If the vote wasn't unanimous, the hitchhiker would go free.

The vote was unanimous.

Wes put on his skull mask. Wes painted his skull mask to look real, with a dark tinted bone of brown. He sanded the eye sockets to appear furrowed and angry.

Tracy walked everyone through what they found in their guest's backpack as Chris and Easton managed the ropes and the guest of honor.

Once ready, Easton cracked smelling salts under the hitchhiker's nose. He startled awake, jerking his arms and legs, but they wouldn't budge. He blinked and shook his head, trying to figure out what was happening. Wes leaned down and slapped the hitchhiker's cheeks.

"Hey, man," Wes said in a gentle voice. "You alright? Are you awake?"

"What is this?" Kenneth asked.

"Kenneth Anderson from Duluth, Minnesota?"

"Yeah, so what? Everyone on the open road lies about their name. What is this? Why can't I feel my—"

"Kenneth, I'm going to need you to shut up and listen to me," Wes said.

"Fuck you, man. Let me go!"

Easton walked where he could watch the entrance of the parking lot. The hitchhiker's voice echoed through the woods surrounding the stop. He didn't know how far his voice might carry.

Wes leaned over the hitchhiker and held up the necklace Tracy put into a plastic bag. He made sure the hitchhiker could see it.

"Samantha McCain went missing three years ago, abducted at a rest stop like this one. Found dead two weeks later, not too far from her car. They never found her necklace. Looked like this one. You know anything about that?"

"No, what are you saying?"

Wes held up a pair of earrings in another bag.

"Jessica Bright. Went missing last year, nearby. Picked up a hitchhiker matching your description. They found her body with unspeakable things done to it. Social media pictures from her trip show her wearing these earrings, but they did not find them on her body."

"Hey, listen, I don't know—"

"I have at least six here to go through. You can admit to what you did or you can deny it. See, the thing is, we know it was you. We're good at this. I'll tell you how we found you. I'll tell you how we know what you did and how we know who you did it to. First, though, we want to tell you exactly the predicament in which you've found yourself. Tracy?"

Wes moved away and Tracy leaned over Kenneth. The night's darkness danced across the teeth of her mask, making it look like a sneering, hideous smile.

"If you look up, you'll see a thick rope."

Kenneth looked up and saw his hands above his head, tied to a thick rope. He nodded. Tears streamed down his face.

"We tied it to the rear of the truck. Now, look down at your chest. We wrapped this rope around your torso. You'll see a rope down there around your waist, tied to your legs too. Not sure if you can see it, but it's there. The other end of that rope trails off into the dark, where it's tied to the biggest tree we could find. When Wes gets in his truck and drives off, the rope tied to your waist and legs will tear you at the midsection. If we're lucky, you'll be alive long enough to feel your torso being ripped in half."

Tracy stepped back as Wes once again took center stage. He leaned over Kenneth and sorted through the plastic bags with the items from his backpack.

Wes outlined everything. He told Kenneth how Tracy had been listening to podcasts and found patterns in what seemed like random cases. She and Britney worked together to build timelines for the women who went missing. They made maps and schedules, had full-blown collages setup in their rooms like a detective on the brink of solving a case.

They looked at public mug shots, police reports, and registered sex offenders near the locations. They searched for reports of hitchhikers in the area. Eventually, they narrowed it down to three people, one of which was missing a mugshot. Thanks to an abandoned Myspace page, they found out the same man in mugshot number two liked to go by the alias of the name belonging to the missing mugshot. Easton spent a few drug-addled nights scouring the internet for bus schedules, train schedules, and comparing notes from the others. It was a lot of work but finding the missing jewelry confirmed it was all worthwhile.

"We know you did what we're accusing you of doing. There's no convincing us otherwise."

Kenneth stared at the stars above. He nodded.

"Yeah," he whispered. "I did it. All of them. There's more. I have names. I can tell you—"

"We suspected there would be others," Britney said. "That doesn't matter to us. Maybe someone will find your body and this evidence and tie it all together. Maybe. But maybe not."

"Britney, why don't you drive?" Wes said, holding out the keys. "I'll keep Kenneth company."

Britney climbed into the truck. It roared to life. Chris and Tracy went into the camper. Easton climbed the ladder and scrambled on top of the camper to be lookout.

"Hey, wait! I can give you names," Kenneth shouted. "I can tell you where to find their bodies."

His words disappeared under the growling of the truck's engine as Britney revved. She pressed the gas. The truck eased forward. After a few feet, Kenneth's arms lifted, then his legs. Soon enough, his body rose off the ground, hanging in midair. His arms stretched out above his head.

"Please!" Kenneth shouted. "Please, don't do this. You're good kids. I can tell."

The truck's engine roared like a beast. It snarled and hollered over the hitchhiker's words, yet eased forward inch by inch. In the breaks between the revving engine, and the spaces between Kenneth's words, Easton heard the rope straining, tightening. After a little more movement forward, Kenneth stopped pleading and grunted and groaned as his arms stretched further out overhead. Britney relaxed the revving of the engine. Wes sent up hand signals, guiding Britney.

"Headlights!" Easton shouted from atop the camper.

Wes ran to the end of the truck and looked over at the entrance as bright white headlights panned out across the rest stop.

Britney reversed to let Kenneth fall back to the pavement, then killed the engine and the lights. Wes ran over to Kenneth and climbed on top of him. He put his gloved hand over Kenneth's mouth. Kenneth's face was sticky with sweat and tears. He whimpered beneath the gloved hand, but only incomprehensible mumbles escaped. Wes pulled out a sharp knife. He stuck the tip of the blade a hair's width from Kenneth's wide open eyeball.

"You make a peep, I'll slice your eyeballs open," Wes hissed through his mask.

Kenneth whimpered as he tried to move his arms. He stopped making sounds and peeked through the corner of his eye at the headlights as they circled the rest stop.

The headlights swept over the mad scene of the truck and the hitchhiker, though Easton doubted the driver of the car even noticed. They circled around the building.

"We should have closed that damn gate behind us," Easton said to himself. He crawled over to the emergency hatch above the camper's bed. Tracy laid a few feet below, watching the car through the camper window.

The car stopped by the ladies' room and idled out front. It wasn't a cop, much to their relief. The car was a hatchback, fairly new, with a storage shell on top. A ski resort wasn't too far up the road. On the cusp of autumn, the busy season wasn't for another few weeks, so they hoped there'd be less traffic. This was a one off fluke that could cost them everything.

They waited and watched as two young women, the driver and passenger of the car, ran out and into the ladies' room.

"When nature calls," Easton said to himself.

The woods were so silent in the absence of the roaring engine and screaming man. It made Easton wonder how loud they were and who could hear them. Though if a passerby stopped to use the bathroom, they probably didn't hear much.

They watched and waited. The women finally emerged, laughing and talking at the top of their lungs.

"Oh my god, that was so scary," one of them said, their voice carrying across the parking lot.

They meandered over to their car. In the distance, Easton could make out the glowing lights of their phones. There were a few flashes of light in the dark. Easton crawled over to the open emergency hatch on the roof of the camper.

"They're taking pictures," Tracy said. "I hope they don't take a picture in this direction. They'll get the truck."

"They might get more than that," Easton said. "From that angle, they can see Kenneth."

"Shit. We need to get them out of here. The longer they stay, the more likely they'll see us."

"What do you suggest?"

"What if we make Kenneth scream? Scare them off."

"Sure about that?"

"Two women traveling alone in an abandoned and terrifying rest stop hear a man screaming out from the dark? They'll leave. They'll leave and never look back."

"They could call the cops."

"No service for miles."

"They could tell the cops later, have them come back here and find Kenneth's body."

"That's fine."

"Is it?"

"Is it?"

The ladies continued to take pictures and walk around. Easton watched and waited, hoping they'd move on.

His heart dropped as the women walked back to their car. The driver looked up and right at them. She froze and whispered something to her passenger. The passenger walked around the car and they both squinted into the darkness.

"Shit," Easton said. "They see us."

Easton crawled to the rear of the camper and whispered to Wes.

"Scare them off," Easton said. "Make him scream."

Wes took a deep breath and moved his hand from Kenneth's mouth.

"Please, no—"

Wes swiped the sharp blade across Kenneth's eyeball, slicing it open. Kenneth's pained howl echoed through the woods and even made Easton tremble. The women screamed and jumped in their car and peeled out. He let out a sigh of relief as their headlights vanished.

"Let's get this over with and get out of here," Wes said.

"If we weren't doing this right now," Easton said. "It could be those two women he killed next. He was on this road. They were stupid."

"Well, we'll never have to worry about that with this guy again," Wes said.

Wes cleaned the knife on Kenneth's shirt and stepped back, waving for Britney to continue. Britney started the truck, revved the engine and moved forward, inch by inch. Kenneth's arms stretched out again. He lifted off the ground. Still forward, Britney pushed. The rope around his waist went taut and stretched until it tore him in half. Easton wasn't sure at which point Kenneth died. The dark made it hard to see.

Chris and Easton dragged the pieces of him into the woods, not bothering to waste any effort cleaning the spilled blood or the pieces of him. They left his belongings and the evidence of his crimes along with him. Maybe one day someone will find him and the bags of souvenirs he took from the women he killed and put all the pieces together.

"Let the animals have him," Chris said.

They drove off, locking the gate to the abandoned rest stop behind them.

"How much further to Campbell?" Wes asked.

"About four hours and we'll be there," Easton said.

"Can't wait," Wes said with a smile.

After killing Kenneth, Easton went back to the haze, with a cloud of smoke leaking out of the side window of the camper. He turned the table into a bed and watched the trees pass by as they headed to Campbell. Britney left the emergency escape above the bed cracked open to let Easton's smoke out as she and Wes rested on the bed.

Chris took over driving duties. Tracy wanted to drive, but she had trouble seeing over the steering wheel and reaching the pedals, so she sat shotgun.

They drove in an uncomfortable silence. Every so often, when it was safe to take his eyes off the road, Chris stole a look at Tracy as she stared out the window. She was tired but also restless. Bags hung under her eyes. Dark eyeliner smeared across her right cheek, but she didn't seem to care. She stared off, watching the trees fly by, her knees pulled up to her chest, socked-feet resting on the seat.

They had been dating for a year, but Chris confessed to Easton that he felt they knew each other less than before they met. She had grown to be more distant, quieter, less conversational in the past months.

Something changed.

Easton wasn't sure if it was the cross country murder spree, Tracy's father's pending execution or something else altogether. All Easton knew was he couldn't wait for it to end so he could have his best friend back. Of course, with the bloody bond they all shared, their breakup would be easier said than done.

"You alright?" Chris asked Tracy.

Lost in thought, she took a few seconds to register his question. Their voices drifted into the camper and Easton couldn't help but listen.

"What?" Tracy asked.

"You alright?" Chris repeated.

"Do I not seem alright?"

"Doesn't sound like you're alright."

"I'm fine."

"Is it about Kenneth?" Chris asked.

"It's nothing, Chris."

The blankets in the bed rustled. Britney grunted and moaned as she maneuvered on top of Wes.

"Seriously?" Easton shouted at them.

He took a nice long drag from a vape, then eyeballed the open window to the cab. Easton poured through it, determined to get into the backseat of the truck's cab. He spilled out, sprawled across the backseat, then clambered into a seated position in the center. He threw his arms over the front seat and leaned forward.

"Do not leave me alone with them back there ever again," Easton said.

A banging sound came through the roof and from the open window Easton crawled through.

"I thought Wes was tired," Tracy said.

"Well, no one is too tired for that," Easton laughed.

Wes's common boast and complaint was about the number of calories required to maintain "such a physique" as he would say. As a result, their hours-long road trip turned the back seat of the truck into a garbage dump of food wrappers. Easton shoved all the trash in an already overflowing bag and stuffed it on the floor. Lucky for Easton, it was only him in the back and he could lie down and let his high pull him from his own worries. He laid with his head behind Chris in the driver's seat and his socked feet against the cold glass of the rear passenger window.

The truck hummed along. They had been driving for days looking for Kenneth, and their trip wasn't over. Tracy nodded off, her head resting against the window. Chris, not taking his eyes off the road, pulled off his hoodie and draped it over her.

He passed a few big trucks, other campers like theirs and even the car that pulled into the rest stop when they were taking care of Kenneth.

"Easton," Chris whispered, then nodded his head toward the car.

Even though they only glimpsed the car in the dark, it left an unforgettable image in their memory. The occupants didn't seem to recognize the truck. Easton sat up straight to catch a glimpse over Tracy's dozing head and saw the women bickering, wide-eyed and pointing at each other.

Easton imagined they had blown whatever they saw out of proportion. By the time they get to wherever they headed, their story will be even scarier and more far-fetched. The black truck with the camper would probably turn into a creepy van or an RV. The scream will have been blood curdling and ferocious.

Whatever tale they told, Easton felt relief as Chris drove by and they paid him no mind. He even cut them off to make sure they saw him. When they flipped him off and he waved an apology, he knew they didn't recognize him. No one would flip off a vehicle they saw at an abandoned rest stop, accompanied by a grown man's screams.

Miles away from Kenneth's body in the abandoned rest stop, miles further from home, Chris merged onto another long stretch of highway, following signs for a small town in Rhode Island where their next victims awaited.

| 3 |

CROWS

He had taken to killing small animals, crows especially. But he hadn't heard that a crow can recognize a face and so he was unaware of the murder gathering outside his home, waiting for him.

| 4 |

BEFORE THE BODY FELL

A dried-up creek ran along the back of the school where miscreants like me and Dickie liked to hang out. Thinking back, it may not have ever been a creek. The bed had dried up and large trees took over, sprawled out, creating a strip of dried-out jungle running alongside the school. Dead trees and their bare branches reached out in deformed grasps. But at some point it was a creek and so we still referred to it as one.

We weren't delinquents, but we were far from outstanding students. Stoners without all the drugs. Gangsters without all the friends. We were all around fuck ups for no reason at all other than that we were fuck ups. Since no other cliques would have us, we became a little group of social misfits.

Our usual hangout spot in the back of the school was called "Freak Row" where all the goths, punks, and whiny emo kids liked to hang out. This was the heyday of Hot Topic and suburban tragedies, hair-dyed white girls with skinny jeans and studded belts. AOL Instant Messenger was the top-tier form of communication, with Myspace sneaking in, giving those same emo kids a platform. Overhead selfies taken in dim bathrooms with heavy eyeshadow and duct tape over their mouths were becoming the baseline for social normalcy. I never figured out if the wrist decor covered the scars on their wrists or brought attention to it on purpose.

The glory days of self-mutilation for funsies.

My tiny group of friends, myself included, leaned into the skater/punk aesthetic. Long, greasy hair left our faces riddled with acne. We stuffed socks into the front of our skate shoes, wore knee-length cholo socks, and band tees from Hot Topic that were one size too small, adorned with holes rubbed in from our studded belts. I was an early adopter of the ratty, old hoodie before tech bros commandeered the image for themselves. My wrists bore certain scars, covered by a Slayer embroidered wrist sweatband a friend stole from the mall as my birthday gift.

Despite our looks, none of us skated and none of us smoked weed enough to be called a legitimate stoner. Every morning, every ten-minute break, through lunch, and for a few extra minutes after school every day, we would meet and kick around the hacky sack. Kicking it and keeping it up was more fun than we ever allowed ourselves to have once we got home. The endorphins rushing, the sweat, and the fun of it all, as that bean bag flew, left us exhilarated and eager for the next break from our endless studies. Though studies would be a generous term to use for what we did. Teachers often rambled on and on about things we would later look up online when it came time to do the essay.

Meanwhile, Dickie and I took turns drawing dicks and pentagrams in each other's textbooks. The regular beatings for poor grades weren't enough to get me to pay attention to the mindless ramblings of an out-of-touch teacher who saw her heyday in the Reagan administration.

One day, after suffering one of those aforementioned beatings the day before, I wasn't eager to go home for another round of disparaging parental insults. Dickie's parents worked late, and he had to wait for his ride home. He used a local family member's address to go to school in this district, but he lived a little too far for the bus. Another game of hacky sack ended and the others from our group filtered off into their own respective shithole homes, leaving us alone, as often was the case. It was during those late afternoons that we bonded over obscene jokes, offensive impressions, and drawing more dicks into our Spanish textbooks.

We sat on a concrete wall by a small stairwell, letting our feet dangle down. We took turns seeing how long we could let our spit drip before breaking. It was gross, but it was fun for two bored teenagers. At any second, a teacher could come by and yell at us for sitting on that wall and risking injury, then they'd assign us detention for spitting. We'd been there before, a million times. It mattered little, considering both of us were often at school late and it gave us more time to do what we loved to do, draw dicks in books. Detention was a unique chance to steal other people's books and return them filled with dicks without the person noticing.

But that day, none of the teachers came around looking for teenagers to terrorize. Those times in high school, drawing dicks and making fart jokes, were some of the best years I had, until I would go home every day. That escapism meant the world to me. Even though I hated school, I loved being there and I wish I could go back and sit on that concrete wall and spit a loogie at a passing freshman and never have to go back home.

As we spat and sat, I looked out over the chain-link fence, the barrier between the safety of school and the Hell of the outside world. The creek that ran alongside the school was like a moat, guarding the kingdom from the monsters out in the world.

"What are you looking at?" Dickie asked. He moved beside me and followed my line of sight into the trees.

"Do you see that?" I asked.

"See what?"

"It looks like a leather jacket or something. Like someone is standing there watching us. Do you see it?"

"Where?"

"That enormous tree with the small tree next to it. In between those two trees and the tree with the moss on the side of it."

"Dude, what are you talking about? There's, like, a thousand trees out there."

I did my best to point it out to Dickie, but he couldn't figure out where I was pointing. I saw something though, I'm sure of it. It was a brown leather jacket. It might have been hanging on a branch or something. They have kicked out homeless people from that creek before. Maybe one of them made a new camp out there and hung up his jacket. Or maybe, as I thought and what I felt in my gut, perhaps someone was in that jacket, watching us from the trees. An unease filtered through my body and settled in my stomach.

"I don't see anything, man," Dickie said.

"Oh well, whatever. Hey, man, I think I'm going to head home. I have to do some chores before my mom gets home and beats the shit out of me."

"Sure, my dad should be here soon."

Dickie headed off toward the front of the school and I scuttled around to the side and headed home. As I walked, I put on my headphones and blasted music from my portable CD player. I swapped out a few CDs from the binder in my backpack on the way, searching for the best soundtrack to get that creep out of my mind. Marilyn Manson, Slipknot, Kittie, Disturbed. None of them worked to put me into a less terrified headspace.

I threw a glance over my shoulder every few minutes, expecting to see a pedophile in a brown leather jacket walking up the sidewalk toward me. No one was ever there when I turned around. I decided it might be best to put the music away and keep my ears open in case someone tried to run up to me. I wish Dickie had seen it too so he could realize what else it might be other than a guy in a jacket, but he saw nothing. Maybe if he did, he could have helped to put my mind at ease and convince me of something else. Something normal. My obsession with horror comics and true crime books didn't help to stop my imagination from running wild.

When I got home, I checked the house and locked all the windows and doors. Whatever it was, if it was there again the next day, I'd make sure Dickie saw it. As soon as the last bell rang, we'd head over there and jump that fence and go see it up close in person if needed. I did my chores and hid in my room. Footsteps pounded across the floor outside. I held my breath each time, careful not to draw attention and with it, the ire of an angry parent after a long day. The quietest thing I had was a book. So that night, I read about the hauntings of an old New England home and how the ghosts spent generations terrorizing the tenants. I drifted off to sleep with visions of death on my mind and night-mares waiting to terrorize my sleep.

That night, the sound of a knocking at my window ripped me from a deep sleep. I listened out, hoping to hear it again so I could figure out what it was and make sense of it.

My breath and the ticking of the clock in my room were the only things I could hear. I stared at the drawn blinds of my window, too scared to pull it back and see a face looking back at me. Despite waiting and listening, the knocking at the window never repeated. After an, I drifted off to sleep wondering if the sound was real, or a vivid dream.

The all-too-gentle chime of the lunchtime bell rang across campus the next day. We shuffled out of class and headed over to Freak Row, as usual. Sometimes we got lunch. I usually skipped lunch and saved my lunch money. My mom was too worried about how it would look if she applied for the free lunch even though we were broke enough for it. By the end of the month, I'd have saved enough for an action figure, a book, or a CD at the mall. If I was starving, I'd buy a cookie for $0.50 and it would be enough to hold me off until the end of the day. That day, I wasn't hungry at all. I paid even less attention than usual through all my morning classes. All I could think of was the person in the creek. Of course, it had dawned on me by that point that by the time we got there, the person wouldn't be standing there, waiting for the little kid he was creeping on to confront him. He'd probably be long gone, especially if he saw me looking back at him the day before.

But I had to know. I had to see it. Something about it didn't feel right at all.

When I got to Freak Row, there was caution tape up, stopping us from going any further. I met up with Dickie and the others outside the tape.

"What happened?" I asked Dickie, hoping he knew more than I did.

"You didn't hear?" Dickie asked.

"What?"

"Roberto ditched class to get pizza. He cut through the creek and found a dead body."

My heart turned into a heavy piece of burning coal and sunk deep into my gut. The blood rushed from my face and my head snapped over to Dickie.

"Dead body? Are you serious?"

"Yeah, why?"

"Don't you remember? Yesterday? I said I saw someone out there."

"You did?"

"Yeah, remember? After school, I said someone was watching us. Shit, man, what if that was the dead guy?"

"I don't remember that at all," Dickie said.

"Are you kidding? I was up all night thinking about it. Remember? I tried showing you. The trees? I was trying to point out someone watching us between the trees?"

"I have no idea what you're talking about, dude."

It was frustrating, to say the least, but with that seed of doubt planted in my mind, I couldn't help but wonder if maybe I didn't tell him. Maybe it was a dream like the knocking on my window. Maybe I'm already dead and this is all a Hell built specifically for me.

My questioning of myself only lasted a minute. I knew I saw what I thought I saw. There was no way I imagined it. I didn't know what was going on with Dickie.

"Where's Roberto?" I asked, shuffling along to catch up with him, seeming to want none of what I was saying.

As cool as Dickie was, he was sensitive and kind of an asshole. He was the type of dude who liked to play pranks but as soon as the tables turned; he threw a tantrum. One time, Benji borrowed his dad's truck, and I had to climb onto the side to reach the door. As I climbed up and tried to get in, Dickie locked the door. They took off down the street and I was hanging off the side for dear life. Dickie was inside laughing his ass off. Even I laughed when I finally climbed in through an open window. It didn't bother me; it was hilarious. A few weeks later, we were leaving the school parking lot and did the old lock-the-door-and-drive-a-few-feet-ahead to prank Dickie and he got angry and threw his backpack, filled with dick-covered books, at Benji's window. Almost shattered it.

Benji stopped driving us around after that. It was odd. Dickie had the most stable childhood of all of us but was the biggest little bitch out of all of us too. Spoiled, I guess. An overgrown baby who couldn't handle a joke. I wondered if he remembered me pointing something out in the creek. Maybe he saw it, but he didn't want to see it. He wanted nothing to do with whatever was going on. He was the type to throw someone under the bus if it was slightly more convenient to do so than to not. Come to think of it, I don't know why I even hung out with him for so long. I guess he was the only one still around after everyone else left, and I was never eager to go home. Friends by circumstance.

"What happened to Roberto?" I asked again.

"I don't know," Dickie said, raising his voice as if I asked him a thousand times.

I stopped in my tracks and let him walk ahead. He was in one of his moods and I didn't feel like wasting any more time with his prissy bitchassness. I needed to find Roberto.

My next stop was the front office. I didn't know what the consequences were for trespassing and ditching school, but I would imagine finding a dead body would get you off the hook. Either way, a visit to the principal's office seemed warranted and the likeliest place I'd find him.

When I got to the front office, I walked through with no one taking a second look. There were no cops around, which surprised me, but then I guess it made sense. The body was off to the side of the school, not on school property. I got closer to the principal's office but went as far as I could without crossing into the area that was for grown-ups only. I stopped outside and eyed a revolving pamphlet holder with ridiculous options. There were some for ratting out classmates who sell drugs, one for having gay parents, and another for teens who smoke cigarettes, which I thought was pretty funny. It had a picture of a rabbit on it, being neglected by his owner, who was too desperate for a cigarette to clean the rabbit cage. I knew rabbit-owning teens who smoked and there was never any issue with them taking care of the rabbit poop.

My eyes glossed over as I came to the section about jerking off too much and one about avoiding STDs. It felt like the two pamphlets could solve each other's problems, but I wasn't there to make suggestions. I listened out for any news about the caution tape and the dead body. Maybe Dickie misheard.

"...that's so creepy," a voice whispered. "Out in the creek? How'd he do it?"

I couldn't hear how he did it, but I snatched up a pamphlet and pretended to be engrossed in reading it as the principal's door opened and Roberto marched out. An older woman and a cop were talking to the principal as he shut the door behind Roberto. He crossed the grown-ups-only area and sat in the open seats behind me. The entire room went quiet, but only for a moment before the mutters picked back up and everyone pretended everything was normal.

"Hey," I whispered to Roberto. "What happened?"

"I can't talk about it," Roberto whispered back, staring down at his feet.

"Is it true?"

"What?"

"You found a body in the creek?"

"....yes."

"Was he wearing a brown leather jacket?'"

"What?"

"A brown leather jacket. Was he wearing a brown leather jacket? I need to know."

"I don't fucking know, man. I wasn't checking out his wardrobe."

"Excuse me," a voice bellowed.

I looked up and saw the police officer, the principal, and who I assumed was Roberto's mom, walking toward me. The booming voice was the unmistakable voice of Mr. Howard, the principal. I cared little for him, but his voice was beautiful. He missed his calling being a narrator for documentaries instead of being an asshole to students. My blood turned cold as I saw everyone staring at me. Roberto looked back to his feet.

"What are you doing here?" Mr. Howard asked.

"Just needed a pamphlet," I said, holding up the one I grabbed from the rack.

His face turned red, and he averted his eyes. His usual stoic voice fluttered as he excused me. I didn't question it. As I stepped out of the office, I tossed the pamphlet into the trash, but something on the front caught my eye. I stepped back and peered into the trash can. It was a pamphlet about chronic masturbation. I would have been embarrassed if it were further from the truth, but in this case, I felt pretty satisfied and quite happy I didn't grab the bed-wetting pamphlet.

I didn't want to risk another run-in with Mr. Howard. He had a reputation for delivering extensive lectures and imposing his long-winded life views on troublesome students. The last thing I needed was a lecture on masturbation from the principal. Though, with how pale he turned, I doubt it would have happened. Still, there was no sense in risking it. I didn't feel like dealing with Dickie when he was in his little attitude, so I found somewhere quiet and lost myself in a comic book during lunch. After school, I'd bite the bullet and head home to whatever shitstorm awaited me there. Fuck Dickie. He was no help anyway.

The dead body was the talk of the school for the rest of the day. Between the rumors and gossip, what little news seeped out, and whatever the teachers told us, we knew less by the end of the day than we did before. Teachers all pretended not to know anything, but we assumed they were toeing the company line, so to speak. I don't blame them for keeping us in the dark. We were kids. Talking about suicide to a bunch of impressionable young teens, filled with emotion and rage, during the height of cosmetic wrist-cutting and emo dalliance, probably wasn't a good idea.

Roberto, though, became the most popular kid in school. Of all the dumb fucks to stumble across a dead body, it had to be the most aloof dumbass in the entire grade. Take into consideration that each grade in our school was bigger than the last. There were about 5,000 students, with the freshman class being the biggest yet at around 1,200 students. They report that there's a ratio of 23 students to every teacher, but all our classes have over 40 students and a row of people have to sit on the floor in the back of every class. Kind of hard to give a shit about geometry when our legs are falling asleep.

With that in mind, it's hard for a kid in school to stand out among 4,999 others. The so-called popular kids are only popular within their own echo chamber. Step outside their tight-knit circle, and their influence fades; the further they stray, the more their notoriety dwindles. Some students, in fact, might not even know their names. Roberto was the only kid to break that system my entire time there. His popularity was a bit of a phenomenon. He wasn't attractive or cool. He had braces and glasses as thick as goggles. His acne defined his face, and his blazing red hair was greasy and long. His pale skin and scrawny stature allowed him to be the most popular, yet forgettable, kid in school at the same time. Everyone talked about Roberto finding the body, and everyone was his sudden best friend, but nobody even knew who they were talking about when they talked about Roberto.

"I was supposed to ditch with him and get pizza too," a classmate told me after I asked if he heard what happened.

"Oh, really?"

"Totally, man. But I had to stay late in Ms. Piper's class, so I told him to go without me."

"Who's Roberto, again?"

"The guy who found the body."

"No, I mean, what does he look like?"

"You know, Roberto, dude. Roberto."

This guy did not know what Roberto looked like. Anyone who knew Roberto would know Roberto. He's Mexican, but he was as pale and red-haired as Carrot Top. He always said it was some ancestral bullshit. Something about a group of Irish Americans who fought in the Mexican-American War on the side of the Mexicans. But I think his mother fucked around with her red-haired boss.

In middle school, everyone called him Bobbie. He tried to rebrand himself in high school, but in name only. Everything else about him stayed the same way it was before high school. That's what bothered me so much.

I wanted to find the dead body. Instead, the glory went to this loser that no one likes and no one wants to be around. Finding that dead body became his only claim to fame. I'm jealous. I'll admit it. True crime was my salvation, my escape from my shitty home life. It's where I went to keep my demons quiet. I lost myself in the horrific acts of bloody murderers. Serial killers, mafia hitmen, slashers in horror movies, whatever. Instead, fucking Roberto, who nobody knows, finds a body. But he didn't even find it. I did. That's what I saw in the creek. It wasn't someone in a leather jacket watching me. It was the swaying corpse of a dead bum hanging from a tree branch in the woods of the creek. Dickie could have vouched for me, but he's too busy being a bitch. Instead, Roberto is out there hogging all the credit.

By the next morning, the news finally came out in the paper. We didn't subscribe to it or anything. My mom's fingers were far from the pulse of the community, but a house on the way to work had three papers stacked up on their front door, so I snagged that day's from the pile on my way to school. Either the occupant was on vacation or dead inside and rotting away, waiting for their next stop in from the county to check on them. Either way, they wouldn't miss the paper, or stop me from taking it.

I flipped through, letting the unwanted pages fall to the ground, and sneaking the comics page into my backpack. Finally, in the local section, I found it. Despite the rumors and whatever bullshit the school admins tried to spin, they couldn't stop the newspaper from publishing the truth.

The year before, one upperclassman died. In the morning announcements on the school's PA system, they had a moment of silence for her and said she died of a heart condition. Even the school paper said the same thing. But when the city's paper came out, the truth came with it. She died of toxic shock syndrome from not changing her tampon. It's terrible and tragic and gross and heartbreaking for her family for sure, but it was also hilarious to a bunch of asshole teenagers who knew her. She was a piece of shit. She always got into fights and she blamed everything she did wrong on whoever was closest to her. Her best friends hated her in secret, so much so that when they went to the viewing, they snuck a box of tampons into her casket where the parents wouldn't see it. Some rumors said the tampons were a fresh box they shoplifted. Some rumors, the ones I liked to believe because I had my run-in with her, said that the tampons were used.

That was last year's tragedy. This year's tragedy was still unfolding. According to the article, a homeless man, whose name was withheld upon notification of next of kin, was found by a student who was "crossing the creek to get food, which is against the school's policy." The author didn't name the student, obviously, and there's no description of a brown jacket or anything the dead guy wore when Roberto found him. I tore the article out and stuffed it into my binder.

The rumors were still flying that day, but the early momentum of the incident was already running dry. People were admitting to not knowing who Roberto was, subjects changed and conversations meandered away. I zoned out in third period English class as the teacher droned on and on about *The Great Gatsby* and the writer's discussion on the values that drive people's actions. I hadn't read a single word of the book and I didn't plan to. Usually, the class discussions were enough to get me through the tests without doing the reading. If anything, I'd find summaries of the book online the night before a test. Either way, I couldn't pay attention with that damn leather jacket still on my mind. My eyes wandered across the room, first to my secret crush in that class, Andrea. I stared for a moment, but she must have sensed it because her eyes locked onto mine. I tilted my head and stared off into the distance behind her as if it had been what I was doing all along. To play it off, my eyes bounced around the room until I settled on staring out the open door to the classroom. The occasional kid wandered by on their way to the bathroom. The classroom was dimly lit and sad, but outside the sun shined and a cool breeze made its way through campus. Because it was California, the campus consisted of separate buildings, unlike the East Coast schools, which are confined to a single structure, like a prison. As I stared off, as if summoned by my desire, Roberto himself wandered by and off to the nearby restrooms. I raised my hand and got excused to go, stealing one more look at my crush, making sure she wasn't still staring at me. She wasn't. She didn't care, and I didn't blame her. After all, it wasn't like I found a dead body in the creek.

Escaping the mindless rambles of the teacher was as refreshing as the air of the empty campus. Walking around while everyone else was still in class was like entering a hidden world. Sometimes I saw people hanging out without a care in the world, carrying on in conversation like they didn't have anywhere else to be. It made them seem so powerful. I walked between the buildings, meandering my way to the bathrooms, taking my time with each step, and enjoying the fresh air. It must have been how those prisoners felt in *The Shawshank Redemption* when they got to relax on the roof with ice buckets filled with beer. Even though they were still confined in prison, the taste of beer on their lips and the warmth of the sun on their faces made them feel like free men. The monotonous droning on of teachers in other classrooms reminded me of where I was; locked away in a world where everyone is required to obey orders, keep in line, and do as told. Read the books, write the reports, and color inside the lines. There lingered a sense of unease beneath it all. I was a thief, enjoying a stolen moment of peace and autonomy when I should have had none. I was free, for the moment, drinking beer on the roof, making my way to the bathroom to talk about a dead body with a red-haired Mexican kid I've known half my life.

The stale smell of piss and shit brought my wandering mind back to the moment as I stepped into the bathroom and saw Roberto washing his hands. He wasn't making it quick. In fact, he wasn't moving at all. He stood there, staring down at his hands as the water ran over them, spilling down into the sink and spiraling into the drain.

"Roberto?" I called out.

He startled and spun around, face whiter than a ghost and tears pooling in his eyes.

"You scared the shit out of me," Roberto said.

"You alright?" I asked.

"I'm fine."

"I'm surprised you're back so soon."

"My mom thought it would be better for me if I kept to my day-to-day routine. You know, forget about everything and shit."

"Yeah, I get it."

Roberto's hands dripped as he stared at me, on the verge of saying more but holding it back. He turned to the paper towel dispenser and grabbed a few sheets to dry his hands.

"Can I ask you something?" I blurted out.

"No, please. I want to move on. People have been asking me all day."

"I thought I saw something over there the day before."

"What do you mean?"

"I was over on Freak Row and I saw something in the creek. Like a leather jacket or something? Was he wearing that?"

"I don't know. I wasn't checking his outfit."

"Can't you try to remember?"

"No, I want to put it all behind me."

I grab Roberto by his oversized shirt and slam his scrawny frame against the wall. I wrap my other hand around his chin and force him to look me in the eye.

"Listen to me, you little shit. Close your eyes and picture it. Every morbid fucking detail you can muster. Tell me what you see."

"Please, I don't..."

"Now!"

I snarl in his face and feel the heat radiating from my own. I squeeze his face harder and slam him into the wall again. His pale face turns a dark red as he weeps.

"Tell me. Was he wearing a brown leather jacket? You fucking tell me right now you insignificant little piece of shit or the next person to come in here will find a dead body of their own and it'll be your rat-infested, scrawny little corpse."

"I don't know. I don't fucking know!"

His angry shouts squealed. His voice cracked on every other word as he spilled his guts and tears rolled down his face and across my knuckles.

"He was dead, just dead," Roberto continued. "I don't remember his clothes, I don't remember what he was fucking wearing, okay? All I remember is the dead-eyed stare, as if he was looking right at me and into my soul. I froze, and I stared back, right at him. The smell…it's still burned into my nostrils. I slept with menthol rubbed under my nose last night so I can try to get it out of my head long enough to fall asleep. All I can see are his eyes staring up at me from the ground, that noose tied around his neck."

I drop Roberto and step back. He falls to the ground, still crying. Crying harder, shouting louder, telling me everything that he'd been keeping in. I focus on his words as I do my best to keep up.

"His eyes were yellow and bloodshot, his pupils were so large, he looked like a demon who crawled from the pits of Hell. Do you get it? That's all I see every time I close my eyes. Just him, staring at me."

I remembered what it was like, thinking I saw a leather jacket in the woods, not even a face attached to it. Just the jacket alone haunted me more than I thought it would. I couldn't imagine what would have happened if it were me who found him. Would I relish it as I thought, or would I be like Roberto, broken down and crying on the bathroom floor?

"Looking up at you?" I asked.

"...What?" Roberto asked, losing his train of thought at my question. "Yeah, looking up, he was on the ground. The rope, I guess, snapped after he...you know..."

"Where was he? Was he by Freak Row? I swear, I thought I saw a leather jacket and he might have been there when we..."

"No, I was going to the pizza place. Well, I was coming back from there. I had the pizza already, and I was carrying it. There's a hole by the football field in the back of the school. That's where I found him."

"Then why'd they tape off Freak Row?"

"I'm not a cop, dude. I don't know. Maybe they were looking around if there was anything else over there. They didn't find anything that I know of."

"Shit. I thought I saw him before you."

"What? Do you want this? Do you want to see his face every time you close your eyes? Because you can have it. Trust me, if I could, I'd give it to you. Do you want to find a dead body? Be careful what you wish for, believe me. I mean, why would anyone do that to themselves? Who would hang themselves in the woods like that? He was all alone. Dirty. Broken and sad. Then sat there on the ground for days until I found him. What if I never got pizza? What if no one ever found him? You want these questions lingering in your mind? Take them, dammit. Please!"

Roberto moved in and pushed me against the wall this time, screaming in my face with all his worth, jabbing his pointed finger into my chest.

"Why does it matter about a fucking jacket, man? Tell me! Why are you so fucking worried about his goddamn jacket. Why do you want to see him? Tell me!"

"Because I want to know what they'll see when they find me!" I blurted out, screaming back in his face.

We both breathe and step away from each other. Roberto stares at me, wide-eyed and mouth hanging open. I pace back and forth. He sits on the dirty bathroom floor.

"What do you mean?" He asked.

I tried not to look at him, but when I finally did, I broke.

"Look, man," I said, taking a seat beside him on the floor of the bathroom. "People go through shit in life. Sometimes, they should say goodbye to it all. They spend a lot of time in dark places, thinking about things they don't know if they can come back from. It's like a heavy fog that never lifts. No matter what, they can't escape it all. Sometimes people are their own worst enemies. They fight and fight their entire life, and they know they shouldn't be fighting sometimes, but they can't help it. And sometimes, the fight wins and they give up. Sometimes there's darkness that's too overwhelming and the only way to find peace is to say goodbye to it all. Disappear from the world, crawl into a hole, and die. He didn't do it thinking that he could get a good scare out of you. That look in his eyes? It wasn't evil. It wasn't pain and anger. It wasn't any of the horrid things you imagine it was. No. It's peace. It's relief from the pain of everything that followed him through life. Those eyes of his were the windows to his soul, and that was him saying he was sorry for scaring you, but he wanted to let you know he was okay. He was happy for the first time in his life."

"You said..." Roberto began, but his voice trailed off.

"I have these thoughts too. Thoughts that sometimes, I don't know if I can face another day."

The words spilled out and once they started, I couldn't stop them any more than I could stop the tears accompanying them.

"Are you going to...?"

"No. Maybe. I don't know. You know? Sometimes it's all too much. That's why I guess I was jealous. I wanted to know what you saw. I needed to know if I wanted that for myself. I can't stop thinking about it. It's like a yearning I can't stop. Going home is hard sometimes. That's why I hang out with Dickie."

"Yeah, well, Dickie is an asshole."

"Why's that?"

"He talks shit about how poor you are."

"Are you fucking serious?"

"He's an asshole. He talks about how he can't go to movies or concerts because you can't afford to go, but he says it as a joke, like. I'm sorry. I don't mean to pile on your trauma."

"No, you're good. It's all good. It doesn't matter. I mean, it does, but, you know. It's whatever. What an asshole."

Roberto nodded. We sat on the floor in that dungy bathroom with nothing but the sound of a dripping faucet. Elsewhere on campus, my English teacher continued her lecture about Gatsby. The girl I liked looked over and noticed my empty seat. Dickie fiddled with the hacky sack in his pocket. Then there, in the bathroom, I put my arm around Roberto and squeezed him, then made him promise not to tell anyone that I was there for him when he needed someone. We went our separate ways, back to the confines of our dreadful classrooms and the soulless ramblings of our teachers.

That night, as I lay in bed and stared at the ceiling, I felt the heaviness of that day like a warm blanket. Darkness crept in the corners of my mind and that heaviness turned to familiar aches and pains I had known for so long. But something was different this time. I thought about what Roberto must have seen. The dead man's eyes staring at him. I imagined those eyes and thought of the words I said to Roberto. I didn't know where they came from, and at the time I didn't know what they meant, but I knew they were the right words to say. For the first time in a long time, I fell asleep wondering if maybe my future was something worth sticking around to see.

| 5 |

MARY

"Bloody Mary, Bloody Mary, Bloody Mary," she said into the mirror. Satisfied, the bet fulfilled, she turned off the light, ignoring the shadow in her reflection that moved in a way that made no sense as its fingers crawled up to her throat.

| 6 |

TAOTAOMONA WOMAN

Auntie Marie and her kids stayed with us when she came to die. It started small. A seizure first, headaches and blackouts, then memory loss. At first, the symptoms were scattered, so they ignored them. By the time they came to stay with us, she was beyond help and desperate.

During our first dinner, she pointed to her plate and asked what something was. I laughed at first, thinking she was joking, but when no one else did, I told her it was broccoli. The next day, she didn't recognize her daughter, Elizabeth. Elizabeth cried for an hour. She was eight, sweet around the grownups, but had a real mean streak when things didn't go her way.

The tumor changed Auntie Marie's brain, pushing and moving things that shouldn't be pushed or moved. After the memory loss came the hallucinations.

The third night they stayed with us, I woke up to my aunt hovering over me

"...do you?" Auntie Marie asked, ending a question. I missed the beginning.In a daze, I rubbed my eyes and looked around, trying to make sense of the situation. She had taken my room so she could be comfortable. The kids and I set up futons and blankets in the living room. Since I was the oldest and biggest, I got the couch. I looked over to them, checking if any of them were awake or knew what was going on, but all three of them were fast asleep, eyes closed and snoring away. The TV bathed a bright blue across the otherwise darkened room. It murmured in the background, playing reruns of an old show I didn't recognize.

"Do I what?" I asked, still in a daze.

"Do you see the *taotaomona*?"

I felt around the floor for my glasses and slid them on. She came into focus. Her eyes were wide, filled with tears. Frizzy hair stuck out in all directions.

"Auntie, are you alright?" I asked. "C'mon, let's go back to the room."

I slithered off the couch and placed my hand on her arm and led her to the hallway.

"If you see the taotaomona, tell her to go away," she said. "She's making me sick. I need to get better."

"Okay, Auntie, but right now, let's get you back to bed."

A single, dim night light lit the hallway. At the end, my room waited, the door half ajar and darkness inside. As we moved closer, she pulled her arm from my grip and grabbed my forearm, pulling me back, stopping me from walking any further. Her nails dug into my skin. She whispered something in Chamorro but all I understood was, "taotaomona."

"There's no taotaomona," I said.

Taotaomona were a faraway story, spirits found only in Guam. It was a myth to scare kids into behaving. She repeated whatever it was she was saying as she pulled me away from the room.

"Okay, Auntie. I'll check."

I slipped my arm from her grasp, stepped forward and pushed the door wide open.

I scanned the room, but my eyes hadn't adjusted to the darkness. Still, in the dark, I recognized the dresser, Auntie Marie's suitcase and my desk in the corner. I knew where my bed was, but there was something I didn't recognize beside it.

Parts of the room came into focus as my eyes adjusted. I saw the pattern on the blankets, a chair next to the bed. Beside it, the unrecognizable shadow lingered, darker than the other shadows around it. I stepped into the room.

"No, boy," Auntie Marie whispered. "Don't go in there."

I ignored her warnings and walked to the foot of the bed, closer to the shadow, still not making sense of it. Then it moved. Two red circles looked at me, floating and blinking. The eyes were like those of a cat hiding along the treeline, reflecting the light back when a flashlight passed over it. A shiver rolled down my back. My hands turned ice cold. The eyes hovered, blinked, then closed and vanished, taking the shadow with it.

My hand shot out and flipped on the light. Nothing. My bed, the chair, nothing else out of place.

"See, auntie?" I said. "Nothing here. Get some rest. You have an early appointment."

I said the words, but wasn't sure I meant them. I shook my hands to get the blood flowing again. Perhaps it was nothing, a tired mind playing tricks, a half dream influenced by her words.

"Thank you, boy," Auntie Marie said.

She patted my back and waddled past me, looking around, searching for something. Satisfied, she nodded, laid down in bed, and was asleep before I could turn off the light.

If she was imagining things, who's saying she wouldn't get up in the middle of the night and wander out the front door? I decided it would be best to monitor her, so I slept on the floor, or at least I tried to. I couldn't help but stare at the spot over her bed where I saw whatever it was I saw. She called it a taotaomona. The taotaomona live back home in Guam, not here. Not on the mainland.

Back home.

I guess I can't call it that, considering I've only visited once. Auntie Marie's kids were sure to remind me of that every chance they had. They were much younger than I was and not very well behaved. Because of my upbringing on the mainland and my white father, they would often call me "white boy" and "haole". They talked about Guam like everything was an inside joke I wouldn't understand.

"Oh man," Ryan would say. "I miss that restaurant in Tamuning. Have you eaten there? Oh, that's right, you're just a white boy. You're a colonizer."

The eldest, Ryan, was fourteen. He was the leader of the pack. Elizabeth was in the middle, Juan was the youngest at five. Whatever opinion Ryan had, the others reinforced. They would burst into laughter, call me names, and beg me not to colonize them. I'm not sure any of them understood what they were saying.

Even if they did, the things they said couldn't bother me. It wasn't allowed. They needed whatever happiness they could find, even if it was at my expense. The fact of it was, their mother would not get any better. Soon, she'd be dead. The whole family knew it, except her and the kids.

Auntie Marie exhausted Guam's limited medical resources and wanted another opinion from a doctor on the mainland. It was an expensive trip, a 20 hour flight, and a waste of the last days of her life. She burned through whatever little savings her husband left her when he died. Diabetes got him. Another victim of the colonizer's diet.

Everyone in the family saw what she was doing, but we were powerless to stop her. Who could tell someone to accept death, especially someone with children and no husband? Instead of spending her last days with the kids, I was babysitting them while she consulted with doctors who all told her the same thing. The brain tumor was inoperable. It would only get worse. At most, they could make her comfortable.

The morning after the taotaomona incident, my mom asked why I slept on the floor in the room. I told her about Auntie Marie waking me up and what she said about a taotaomona, but I didn't tell her what I saw. I wasn't even sure if it was real, so I kept that part to myself.

"What's wrong?" I asked.

"Nothing. What do you mean?"

"Mom, what is it?"

"I'm sure it was nothing. She's having a hard time."

My mom shooed me away to take my cousins to the park down the street.

The next night, I slept on the floor in my room again to monitor Auntie Marie. I spent most of the day keeping the kids distracted, so I was exhausted and ready to sleep.

A few hours into the night, I woke and sat up in bed, unsure why. A little alarm clock across the room glowed a dim yellow. I squinted to see the time. Two in the morning. Auntie Marie's rhythmic breathing filled the room, but another sound got my attention. There was a creaking noise I recognized. The chair next to my bed made that sound whenever I got up. It must have been what woke me. I laid back and looked straight ahead, under the bed and through to the other side. Shadows moved.

I sat back up and stared over the bed. Auntie Marie groaned in her sleep and rolled over toward me. Beyond her, my eyes drifted. They looked at the familiar shadows and then once again settled on the shadow I didn't recognize. Two red eyes centered in the mass of darkness looked at me and blinked. They floated up and down, as if nodding to me. Then they turned back to Auntie Marie, who was still asleep. The eyes stared, unmoving.

"*Hafa adai*," I whispered.

The eyes snapped back to me and stared.

"She said to leave her alone. You're making her sick," I said.

The shadow moved around the eyes, but the eyes didn't move. The longer I stared, the more it came into focus. It was a woman. She was tall and wide. Her hair was long, it dragged on the floor and had hibiscus woven throughout.

The red eyes blinked, then vanished, and so too did the shadow woman. I checked under the bed, but I saw nothing there. No recess or corner of the room hid any indistinct shadow or red eyes.

I told myself I was still asleep and that it was only a dream. It had to be, so I laid back down and before long, I drifted back to sleep.

I dreamt of ghosts hiding in the jungle. The shimmering eyes of taotaomona blinked on and off throughout the trees like the twinkle of stars in the night sky. They called to me in familiar voices, laughed like children, and screamed like beasts.

The cacophony of noise from the jungle faded into the banging of dishes from the kitchen. I woke to the smell of Spam and eggs.

The bed was empty.

From the kitchen, Elizabeth shouted Ryan's name and Auntie Marie chided him. My arm tingled. I thought I slept on it wrong, but when I looked down, from my elbow to my shoulder, everything was purple and blue. I poked it and winced at the pain.

I made my way to the kitchen and sat between the boys as they fought over food. I snatched the last stack of thin-sliced and crispy Spam and a mouthful of eggs. My mom and Auntie Marie were talking about a cousin of theirs and the drama she had gotten herself into with a woman who moved to Santa Rita, the village where my family lived on Guam. Elizabeth had her mom's phone and was busy watching baking videos. She didn't bother looking up until Auntie Marie let out a piercing scream.

My blood turned ice cold at the sound. The hair on my arms stood on end and chills shot through my body. Juan burst into tears and wailed. Ryan stood up and rushed to his mother's side. Her finger hovered, outstretched, pointing at me.

"What happened to your arm?" My mom asked.

"I don't know," I said. "I woke up with a bruise."

"Taotaomona," Auntie Marie said. "Taotaomona!"

She repeated the words, getting louder with each repetition until she turned belligerent, screaming, "Taotaomona! Taotaomona!" as loud as she could. She stumbled backward off the chair and fell to the floor, pointing at my arm as she scooted away. Tears flowed down her cheeks, and she screamed the words again and again.

"Taotaomona! Taotaomona!"

"Go! Get out of here. You're upsetting her," my mom said, waving me off. "Go put a long sleeve on."

I ran to my room and shuffled through the clothes hanging in my closet until I found a hoodie and pulled it on. My hands trembled when I pushed them through the sleeves. She wasn't pointing at me; she was pointing at the bruise on my arm. A taotaomona bite. I wanted to excuse it all away as part of her sickness, but I couldn't. The shadows were as real to me as the bruise on my arm.

The room was still dark. I didn't bother with a light since I knew my way around. From the corner of my eye, I saw something move. I spun around and searched the room but found nothing. As I turned and made for the exit, I almost tumbled over Juan and Elizabeth. They were standing outside the door. Elizabeth had her arms around Juan and they were both in tears.

"Are you guys alright?" I asked.

Elizabeth sniffled and nodded, then glanced back toward the kitchen. We couldn't see into the kitchen from where we stood in the hallway. She wasn't screaming anymore, just muttering the words to herself loud enough to carry through the hallway. Ryan and my mom tended to her.

I wrapped my arms around them both and squeezed them tight. They might not have understood what their mom was going through, but I did. I think I needed to hug them more than they needed my hug. In the empty room behind me, something creaked the way the chair next to the bed creaked. I kept my eyes on the kids and made sure they didn't look behind me.

"Hey, you guys want to go do something? We can go to the park, the mall. We can go to a movie."

They shook their heads at all the suggestions.

A loud bang brought their attention back to the kitchen. I ran over and saw a chair lying on its side. Auntie Marie's eyes were closed. She hugged my mom. Her clothes clung to her, hair ran across and stuck against her sweaty face. Tears ruined her morning mascara. I picked up the chair and moved it away from Auntie Marie's foot so she couldn't kick it over again.

"I'm going to take the kids to the mall," I said. "Ryan?"

Ryan looked at my mom, who nodded, then Ryan kissed his mom on the forehead and followed me. His shoulders slumped. The usual snarkiness was nowhere to be found.

We spent the day walking around the mall, then watching a movie that was longer than any of us wanted it to be. The kids were quiet. I wasn't sure how much they understood what their mother was going through. My own thoughts wanted to run wild, but I kept them in check to make sure the kids were alright.

We stopped at the park after the movie. As soon as we got there, Juan sprinted to the playground and found a group of kids. Ryan headed over to the courts to see if anyone was playing basketball. Elizabeth made her way to the swings. Instead of swinging, she dug her toe into the sand and pushed herself from side to side. She stared at the ground. With each small swing, the chains let out a massive groan. Even if I wanted to pretend everything was alright, I couldn't ignore the chains begging for help.

"What's wrong?" I asked.

She jumped at the sound of my voice. I guess she didn't hear me approaching. She stared at me on the verge of tears but fought to stop herself from crying.

"Are taotaomona real?" Elizabeth asked.

Before I could answer, I heard Ryan's snide voice interrupt. The courts must have been empty.

"How would the white boy know?" Ryan said. "Taotaomona only show themselves to true Chamorros. Besides, they stay on Guam."

"Ryan, this isn't the time," I said, but he didn't care.

"Back home, mom locked her door at night. She said it was so the taotaomona wouldn't hurt us, but she didn't lock her door here because she said the taotaomona wouldn't leave Guam."

"Have you seen the taotaomona?" I asked.

"It's not real," Ryan said. "She's going crazy."

"Don't say that," Elizabeth said.

"It's true! Mom's crazy. She sees things. I wish she would die already."

"Ryan!" I shouted.

The dam burst and Elizabeth's tears poured down her cheeks. She jumped off the swing and stormed toward the playground. Ryan's look of triumph faded as she sat on the bottom of the playground steps and held her face in her hands.

"You can't talk like that," I said to Ryan. "Especially not to Juan and Elizabeth."

"We all know she's dying."

"You're right, you know. She's going to die. Soon. You're the big brother. It doesn't matter how you feel. What matters is how you make them feel. It'll be up to you to take care of them. You'll be all they have left. Go over there and make her feel better. Now."

I stomped away, back to the bench. It took Ryan a few minutes, but he made his way over to Elizabeth and put his arm around her. He glared at me as he spoke to her. After a few words, he moved so I couldn't see his face, but it looked as if he cried with her.

We headed home in time for dinner. I put on a movie for the kids in the living room and laid out the pizza for them with paper plates and napkins, then joined my mom in the kitchen.

"How is she?" I asked, keeping my voice down.

"As you'd expect," my mom said. "It's hard. I don't know how much longer she has. It's getting worse every day. She's just going around wasting time and money looking for someone who can do the impossible."

"Does she have any more appointments?"

"She should spend time with her kids, not going to doctors. The doctors can't do anything. They keep telling her that."

My mom finished her slice and poured a shot of Jack into a cup and mixed it with cola.

"How are you holding up?" I asked.

She had me when she was young, and we spent most of my life without my dad. It was always us against the world. She was tough, but sometimes I forgot she could feel pain. It couldn't be easy watching her sister waste away like that, especially when she had to hold it together for the sake of the kids. Auntie Marie's impending death hung over our heads like the blade of a guillotine waiting to fall.

My mom stared down at the empty plate and let out a deep sigh. She stared for so long I wanted to reach out and shake her and see if she was alright. When she looked up at me, tears ran down her cheek and she burst into full sobs.

I held her as she wept. She tried to stop herself from crying, flexing her face, holding the tears back. Chamorros have been through so much. We aren't allowed to cry, especially not the Chamorritas.

"Mom?" I asked. "What was that this morning? Her screaming about taotaomona?"

My mom pulled away from my hug. She had stopped crying and wiped away the tears that escaped. I was wearing a t-shirt again; the hoodie was too hot for the California heat. She stared at the bruise on my arm.

"You know what a taotaomona is," she said.

"Yeah, spirits of ancestors living in the jungle of Guam. During the Spanish occupation, it became a way to look to the past and pay respect to—"

My mom raised her hand and shook her head.

"No. Don't analyze it. I know I haven't been able to give you the upbringing I would have liked. We let our traditions fade, but you need to understand. This is culture. You need to be respectful or it can hurt you."

I nodded and let her continue.

"When your auntie was little, something bad happened to her. Around that time, the base on Guam was expanding, and needed to cut down trees. The man who hurt your aunt was in the military. I guess he was working on the crew that cut down those trees. He fell ill. Abrasions and welts covered his body. His throat swelled up and filled with blisters, which eventually burst. He ended up choking to death on his own blood. The doctors said he had an extreme allergic reaction, but we knew the truth. It was the taotaomona. Not only did he disrespect them by cutting their trees, but he hurt a Chamorrita. The *suruhåna* said that the taotaomona may have been a direct ancestor of Auntie Marie's and was getting payback.

"Taotaomona protect the jungles and the ancestral lands but sometimes they help people. It's why your grandpa is so old yet so strong. He says the taotaomona give him their strength when he needs it. Sometimes a taotaomona could be a protector too."

"If it's protecting her…"

"Taotaomona can make people sick. Not on purpose. They don't mean to, but sometimes it happens. That's how it is."

I nodded and finished my pizza crust.

"Believe what you want," my mom said. "After the soldier died, your auntie had nightmares of a taotaomona woman watching her sleep. The same woman, every night."

I felt the same icy chill in my veins that I did the first night I saw it. Goosebumps prickled across my skin.

"She said she saw the taotaomona's eyes, they would—"

"Red eyes," I said, cutting her off. "Red eyes that shimmer in the light like a cat's. She's large, like Auntie Noreen. Bigger. Taller too."

"That's… Did she tell you?"

I shook my head.

"I saw her."

"What do you mean?"

I told my mom about the two nights I saw the taotaomona woman and how it blinked, then vanished. My mom's hands trembled, yet she shook her head and pursed her lips.

"No, you were tired. Your mind was playing tricks on you. The brain tumor, the doctors said it's causing mental problems. 'Neuropsychiatric' is what they called it. She can't think straight. It must have been there for a while."

"Mom. No. I saw it. Clear as day. I mean, how else would you explain the bruise on my arm?"

"Maybe you bumped it, I don't know."

"Mom."

She waved her hands in front of her face to say she was done with that nonsense.

"Sleep in the living room with your cousins tonight. Let your auntie rest."

She went to watch TV with the kids. My mom believed in things when it was convenient for her, but whenever it had to, her Catholicism triumphed and everything else was a folk tale. I stood alone in the kitchen, looking down the hall at the half ajar door to a quiet room with a dying woman.

Auntie Marie's condition worsened in the following days. We checked her in at a hospital where they promised to make her comfortable but made sure we understood there was nothing they could do to stop the inevitable.

She died in her sleep, her children at her side.

I wondered if the taotaomona woman was there too.

The next few days were hard. It didn't stop Ryan from making fun of me for being born on the mainland. He did it with less enthusiasm, and the others didn't laugh when he did it. It was a comfort, bringing a sense of normalcy in an unsure time.

My mom worked on getting the kids and their mother's body back to Guam. We found a place for them to stay with a cousin. He would serve as more of an extended babysitter than a father figure. From there on, they were on their own.

While they were gone one day, I did something nice for them. By then, they'd been away from Guam for a month. They were tired, sad and homesick.

I rolled dough for titiyas into uneven circles and cooked them on a skillet. Adding a twist of my own which incorporated lemons, I baked soft white cake and let it cool for dessert. Once the red rice was cooking, I headed outside and grilled the finadene-marinated chicken. I set a few chicken thighs aside, diced them up and mixed them with calamansi and onions for the kelaguen. Just before they arrived, I finished the white cake with custard for homemade latiya, and added a sprinkle of cinnamon and a dash of lemon zest.

They got home in the late afternoon, ragged and tired from a day of what must have been stressful for my mom and exhausting for the kids.

"What smells good?" Elizabeth asked.

"I'm hungry," Ryan said. "What's for dinner?"

"Wait, is that red rice?" My mom asked.

They made their way into the kitchen. My cousin's eyes went wide. Across the counter, I displayed all the Chamorro food I put together. I handed Ryan a plate.

"Dig in," I said.

And they did.

They devoured the chicken, obliterated the red rice, and shoveled kelaguen into their mouths on corn tortillas. By the end of the meal, nothing was left but a small piece of latiya that Ryan and I fought over. I let him win, but not without a fight.

We sat back, rubbing our full bellies.

"That was so good," Ryan said.

"Yeah?" I asked. "Do you know how to cook Chamorro food?"

"No," Ryan said.

"Reminds me of home," my mom said with a smile.

"Me too," Elizabeth said.

"Good job, *Chamaole*," Ryan said with a smile.

"Chamaole" was a word that got thrown around a lot in our family. It combined Chamorro and haole for people like me who were half white. From anyone else, it was an insult. From Ryan, it was a step up from "white boy." I smiled in return.

I saw a change in Ryan. The dishes piled up, so he washed them with no need to be told. He helped Elizabeth and Juan get ready for bed and even read a bedtime story to them. When they first showed up, I wished for him to stop joking for five minutes. Given everything, I'd wish twice as hard for anything that would get a chuckle out of him.

We hugged goodbye at the airport. I didn't want to let them go. I couldn't imagine what they were going through. My mom planned to escort them home with her sister's body, then she'd stay for the rosaries and funeral. We couldn't afford a ticket for me. I haven't been to Guam since I was a kid and I wondered if I'd ever make it back again.

I told them not to be strangers and that I'd miss them and I think it was true. We were off to a rough start, but as the days came and went, we grew closer. We were family, not strangers from opposite ends of the globe. I wasn't a colonizer; I was a cousin. I wasn't a white boy; I was a Chamaole.

That night was the first night I slept in my bed again since I relinquished it to Auntie Marie. It was the first time I slept in my room since the taotaomona woman bit my arm and bruised it. The more I thought about it, the more I thought my mom was right. Maybe it was in my head. I didn't sleep well in the living room and maybe the sleep deprivation made my mind play tricks on me.

I remembered a piece of art I came across a long time ago that showed two red eyes glowing from behind a latte stone among a backdrop of ferns and trees. I was never really sure if I believed in taotaomona or considered it to be an old myth from "back home" that my mom told.

An old *National Geographic* had pictures of Chamorritas. One picture was of a large woman grating a coconut. When I was little, my mom told me the woman was her great-grandmother. She kind of looked like the taotaomona woman. It made sense. She wanted to protect my aunt, her great-granddaughter.

If she were real, that is.

Perhaps I combined the two images and let Auntie Marie's words influence my sleepiness.

The last month had been hard, so I tried my best to push those thoughts from my mind to get a full night's sleep. The chair beside my bed creaked. I forced my eyelids open, but they were heavy and my mind had already begun to dream. As my eyelids fell, I could have sworn I saw a dark shadow move, two red orbs staring at me, but then it blinked and it was gone.

| 7 |

WINE

The wine tasted of floral and oak but beneath those flavors lied an unrelenting taste of metal which lingered on her tongue. The poison was too far into her system, she gasped for air but none came.

| 8 |

THE GUARDIAN MAN

Peter Price's costume itched underneath his clothes, his cape bundled between his shoulder blades. He pushed through the dense crowd of tourists at Pier 39, worried another character had already taken his spot. It was the prime location in all of San Francisco for costumed characters, right at the edge of Pier 39, among a dozen restaurants, gift shops, and tour bus lines where bored tourists with money to burn gathered.

On a good day, Peter took home a few hundred in cash. He could pass a thousand a day leading up to Christmas. Today was the last day of a three-day weekend, culminating in July 4th. Locals and visitors alike found their way to the piers and waited along the water to watch the ever-famous fireworks display to celebrate American Independence.

Of course, it was the day Peter overslept.

The crowds were already there, arms full of shopping bags, bellies filled with fried seafood. As Peter navigated through a group of elderly tourists, he caught a break in the crowd and slipped through.

Someone had already taken his corner. A giant ogre from an animated movie posed for pictures with a group of cheerleaders from Montana, who tipped generously after each photo—money that should have been Peter's.

"C'mon, man," Peter said to the ogre once the cheerleaders walked away. "You know this is where I usually work."

"Hey, you snooze, you lose," the ogre said. "You know the deal. Just because you usually have the spot doesn't mean you own it."

Peter knew, but he was hoping for a courtesy considering the ogre, Jonas is his real name, spent the last six months in jail for fighting a fluffy unicorn man in front of a school bus full of kids.

Peter didn't want to fight, especially not with Jonas. While rough around the edges, Jonas was genuine in trying to better himself. He had five kids at home from three different mothers, all chasing him for child support. Despite his irresponsibility, Peter admired how Jonas was with his kids. He was a noble father, and playing a character helped keep his children clothed.

Peter nodded, letting Jonas know he understood. The other characters had already claimed the second and third best spots, to the fifteenth. Peter would have to move about half a mile away from the pier. There was an unwritten rule among the characters not to perform or pose too close to one another unless they were from the same franchise.

Peter made his way to the other side of the pier. On that side, exhausted families who had parked too far away walked in the scorching sun to reach the pier. They were usually grumpy from trying to find parking, regretting their visit because of the costs, and hoping their cars wouldn't get broken into—a genuine concern and a likely event.

Meeting tourists on this side of the pier meant encountering them before the magic of the city put them in a good mood. As he approached his spot, he made a show of getting into character.

When Peter first considered joining the characters in San Francisco, he had considered nothing other than the one character who meant the world to him: Guardian Man. Guardian Man was the strongest, fastest, high-flyingest superhero that ever graced the pages of a comic book, a tv set or the silver screen. He is the hero's hero, and more than that, Peter bore an uncanny resemblance to the actor who played Guardian Man in the 1990s television show. Not to mention they shared a first name.

When Peter went to work, he didn't wear his costume outright but dressed as the mild-mannered reporter Peter Powers, with the hidden uniform of Guardian Man beneath. As he circled his spot, he nodded at the passing tourists who made eye contact.

Finally, he pointed to the sky and began his routine. While the other performers had their signature acts, none compared to his. He spent months perfecting it, practicing day and night before debuting it for an audience, where it always earned applause. The first time he performed, he was nervous. His hands trembled, but he kept his composure. With each performance since, he improved, his confidence growing stronger every time.

"Up in the sky," he bellowed. "What is that? A meteor? Or perhaps a giant robot looking to tear San Francisco apart?"

He ripped the hat off his head and threw it to the ground, then loosened his tie and pulled it from his neck.

"Fear not," he continued. "For I am not the man you assume me to be. I am a hero, a true savior, and I will protect the lovely people of San Francisco."

He pulled open his shirt. The buttons were magnets for this very reason, revealing the giant red "G" on his chest, vibrant in contrast to the purple undershirt. He threw the shirt to the ground.

"For I am Guardian Man!"

He ripped off his pants—magnetic, too—and tossed them with the rest of his clothes.

"I am here to rescue the day and take photographs with the people I save. I work on tips."

A small scattered applause sounded through the crowd, and a few people snapped pictures. To him, it was thunderous applause and the little camera phones were flashing lights of paparazzi, gathered to capture the heroic moment of Guardian Man's saving of San Francisco. He beamed with pride and his perfect white teeth shined.

Tourists passed by, some asked for pictures and offered tips. It was less than he would have gotten had he woken up on time and made it to his favorite spot, but the ogre was right, he snoozed and lost.

The day went on; the sun rose high in the sky. He spent half his morning's earnings on cold water and a hotdog from a street vendor. A few more tourists trickled by, pointing him out to their friends, but only a handful asked for photographs, and not all offered tips.

"You make good money doing this?" a voice asked.

Peter turned, ready to interact with another customer. His smile faded, and he turned red. He didn't recognize the voice but knew the face. A video had circulated a few months prior showing this man in a denim vest beating another character and robbing him. Known to rip people off now and then. The cops never paid much mind; to them, the characters were an equal nuisance.

"Not really," Peter said. "It's more for fun than anything."

"So you don't mind if I take this," the man said, not asking, but stating it as a fact.

Peter hesitated and considered his options. Over the mugger's left shoulder was an obvious lookout. Both were bigger than him. Despite his love of heroes, he knew he wasn't one himself. He had never been in a fight and never planned to be.

"Seriously?" Peter said.

"I never kid."

"Of course," Peter said, his voice small and defeated. He waved them over to the hat on the ground with a few dozen crumpled up dollar bills. "Like I said, this is more fun than anything."

The mugger helped himself. Peter shook his head but did nothing as the man laughed and shoved the cash into his pockets. A few passersby glanced over, but most of them knew what was happening and looked the other way. The city was a harsh place, known to be more harsh in the last few years than it had been before. The characters knew this, and they took the risk. But it was better to let them have the money than to put up a fight and ruin some kid's childhood as they get beaten into the ground dressed as a favorite character. The men took the last few coins and disappeared into the crowd, leaving behind a dime and a nickel. Peter watched until he couldn't see them anymore, then stared off into the distance. Tears welled in his eyes, his face flush with heat. He shook his head, forcing himself back to the moment.

A small boy stood a few feet away, watching. He was young—Peter guessed about six or seven, the target demographic for someone like him. And he had witnessed Peter get robbed. The boy had messy hair and dirty shoes, a backpack slung over his shoulders.

Peter nodded at him and forced a smile. The boy grinned back, revealing missing teeth. Peter pictured the tooth fairy taking them. The boy rummaged through his backpack and produced a Guardian Man comic book, holding it up. Peter's smile widened, this time his heart was in it.

"Do you want a picture?" Peter asked.

The boy balled his hands into fists and held them at his chest, squeezing them tight, trying to contain the excitement bubbling up inside him. A sparkle of joy danced in his eyes, and he bounced on the balls of his feet, unable to stay still. As he stepped forward, a heavy hand landed on his shoulder and pulled him back. An older woman in a janitorial uniform wagged her finger.

"I'm sorry," she said. "We don't have any money."

Peter's heart sank at those words. As much as he needed the money, and despite the fresh wound of being robbed, he hated that this young boy's interaction with Guardian Man had been so quickly tarnished by the mention of money.

"Don't even worry about it," Peter said. His eyes wandered over to his empty hat. "It's a holiday. This one is free."

"You sure?"

"Cross my heart..." Peter said, dragging his finger in an X across his chest. "This would make my day as much as I hope it would make his."

She waved her son over and snapped a few photos. Peter broke out his more rehearsed poses that he usually saved for birthday parties. As the mother snapped away, the anger and frustration of the wasted day slipped away. Sleeping in, losing his spot, getting robbed of his earnings didn't matter. All that mattered were the photos this little boy would have to cherish for the rest of his life. After a few minutes of photos, the little boy hugged Peter's leg, then they took off with a flurry of "thank you's."

The fireworks started with a loud explosion high in the sky. He turned and watched as the colorful sparks fizzled out. The show had begun. The fireworks boomed and thundered across the bay. Tourists made their way to the edge of the water, forgetting about people like Peter. He collected his near-empty hat, occupied only by the nickel and dime left behind, and the pieces of his Peter Powers costume and changed back into his secret identity to make his way home.

Along the way, he ran into other characters, retiring for the night, heading to the trains. The ogre caught up to him, his head under his arm like a basketball player carrying his ball home after a day of hoops. He stuffed the rest of his costume into a gym bag and slung it over his shoulder. He flaunted a handful of cash to a few of the other characters who joined in on the walk to the train station. They ignored the backsplash of fireworks exploding over the bay.

"Hey, no hard feelings, right?" Ogre asked.

"I'm setting three alarms tonight," Peter said.

"Can I buy you a beer?" Ogre asked.

"Thanks, but Guardian Man doesn't drink."

"Okay, but does Peter drink?"

"Not in costume."

"You're not in costume anymore."

"Ah, but I am."

Peter popped open his top button on his shirt and shows off the bold "G" logo on his chest and adjusts the lensless glasses that complete the costume.

"Well, maybe another day," Ogre says.

Ogre picks up the pace. The rear foot of his costume hangs out of the large duffel bag slung over his shoulder.

They have to consider the neighborhoods they go through, the train ride and dealing with drunks and college kids. There's no shame in being a character. It's fun. They all love what they do and for those out on the pier, they get to be their greatest heroes. And ogres.

But on the train ride, or walking through the city, they could get stopped for pictures, which is a big no-no according to the new laws set by the city. They could come face to face with a drunk who decides his bad day is the fault of the animated character staring him down on the bus. Whatever comes across an imaginative mind has happened enough for them to strip their costumes and make their way home as civilians with ogre feet sticking out of their bags.

That's also why Peter considered himself to be the smartest of them all, with his secret identity costume. Joined in the group are out of costume heroes like Guardian Man's annual team up partner, The Mercenary. There's also Wo-Man, Batfreak, Swordwoman and Underwater Dude from the same universe as Guardian Man. Then there's the fantasy characters, witches and warlocks and another ogre, but this one is blue. The group grows, then shrinks as people peel off and head for home. Some of them make their way over to their night jobs where they earn the money that actually goes toward their bills. The walk is about twenty minutes and at last, Peter ends up with a handful of characters as they near the train station, including his least favorite, another Guardian Man.

"Hey, Guardian Man," Guardian Man said to Peter for the thousandth time.

"Hey Doug," Peter said.

"Hey, man, where's the courtesy? It's Guardian Man," he said for the thousandth time as well, before an exaggerated laugh.

Peter is never sure if Doug is mocking Peter's dedication or has a poor sense of humor. Either way, Peter didn't enjoy sharing the Guardian Man limelight with someone so crass. Where the others stripped their costumes, Doug always wore his home. Once, an officer on the train tried to make him change, so he stripped down to his tighty-whities and made a complete affair of it, accusing the cop of sexual assault. A video of the incident went viral, and people say the police were told to leave Doug alone after that.

Peter and Doug were the last of the characters as the train pulled into the station. Doug lit a cigarette.

"I'll catch the next one," Doug said, holding the smoke and then letting it drift out from his nose.

"You shouldn't do that," Peter said.

"Yeah, that's what my doc says."

"No. I mean it. Stop. Put it out right now."

"What are you talking about, man?"

"There are kids here. Kids who look up to Guardian Man. You shouldn't be smoking in costume. They'll think it's cool and then they'll start smoking."

"C'mon, man. Do you really believe that shit?"

"Guardian Man doesn't swear either."

"C'mon, it's been a long day and you want me to not smoke and not cuss? That's stupid."

"Seriously, you're giving us a bad name. Not just that, but I'm also Guardian Man. You're making me look bad by association."

"Get off it, man. You're not my mother. I come out here to get away from people telling me what to do. I don't need you riding me too."

A kid passed by, staring at Doug. He whispered to his mom. She smiled and nodded, then her smile faded and she whispered something back, then hurried him away.

"Where are you going, mom?" Doug calls after her. "Don't you want to know what Guardian Man is all about?"

"Doug," Peter said.

"Guardian Man."

"I'm not calling you that. Not while you smoke, you shout obscenities, you harass — Have some respect for the costume."

Peter's face burned. The words stumbled on their way out of his mouth.

"Get on the damn train, and get off my back, Peter. I swear. I'm so sick of your uppity bullshit."

The train horn bellowed behind him and hissed to a halt. Peter smelled the stale air before even boarding. He turned to the train without another word and climbed aboard.

Getting to his seat, he looked out the window where Doug posed for a picture with a group of drunk college kids, all sticking up their middle fingers. Doug too. Peter shook his head. The train doors closed. Doug faded away, waving his finger at Peter, then vanished in the distance behind him as the train moved on.

Peter kept to himself in the back of the crowded train. A little boy passed wearing a Guardian Man shirt. Peter smiled at the boy and debated on showing him the shirt beneath his secret identity. He pondered for too long and the boy's mother hurried him away, shooting an ugly look at Peter's direction.

Peter took the train across the Bay. People came and went, and as the train neared the last stop, he was the only passenger left. He felt guilty that the train operator had to make the last leg of the journey just for him, but also felt a certain specialness in having the train all to himself. He rose from the sticky seat, leaving behind the smell of recycled air and age-old piss.

His journey wasn't over yet. He hurried across the platform, down the stairs, across the street, and rushed to catch the bus.

He once had a regular job. He was the Head Technical Data Analyst II for a tech startup that processed home insurance claims and managed home loans. It was dreadful and boring in every way. After six years, a competitor bought the company. The CEO and managers made enough money to retire early, while they laid off everyone else without warning.

After that, Peter decided to never work for anyone else again. The dim lights, the senseless chatter, the office drama—it was all more than Peter could stand. Although a payout would have been ideal, getting let go was a blessing in disguise.

He made his first Guardian Man costume for a Halloween party. It was such a hit that he made another one, improving his skills with each new version. He hid his fifth costume beneath his Peter Powers secret identity outfit, which he tailored himself from clothes purchased at a vintage thrift shop.

Whenever a new movie or TV show came out, he updated his costume. No one wants a picture with Guardian Man from three movies ago; they want the new, updated Guardian Man who saved San Francisco and defeated Dr. Corrupto.

Being Guardian Man for kids who love the movies or for tourists seeking an authentic representation of America is the most fulfilling job Peter has ever had. He'd rather die than spend another day scrolling through spreadsheets and incalculable data.

The bus stops in downtown San Jose, and he walks past the closing bars and through a college campus to get home. His Peter Powers disguise makes him stand out: a tweed suit, a fedora, and thick-rimmed glasses without lenses. Combined with the rising summer heat, he seemed either distinguished or mentally ill.

Loneliness followed him. Even when channeling Peter Powers or Guardian Man. He imagined if Peter Powers or Guardian Man were real, they would also feel lonely. They were alien entities, human in appearance only, but gifted incredible powers by a sorcerer on their home planet. Their power was too strong, so their planetary guardians sent them away to die in deep space, but they crash-landed on Earth instead. They walked among those they protected, those who feared and hated them, risking their own safety to keep humans from harm.

For once in his life, he was a hero. The looks of admiration Guardian Man received when he saved the day were as rewarding as the looks of awe from children who took pictures with Peter.

Peter took a left down a business sector where dark alleys dotted the road. The streetlights here didn't turn on because there were no pedestrians at night.

None except Peter.

And that night, there was a commotion ahead.

He walked, perking up his ears and listening to the sounds of that normally quiet street. There was something painful about what he heard. As he walked, he carefully stepped past each alley, not sure from which alley the noises came.

As he inched toward the corner, he peeked out. It took a second for his eyes to adjust, but as they did, the scene came into focus and his heart leapt into his throat.

A van with an open back door idled a few feet away from Peter. At the end of the alley was an open back door to the business. Two women knelt on the ground with their hands in the air, huddled together wearing janitorial aprons. A man stood over them. Tall and built like a linebacker. He aimed a gun at them. A second person strolled out of the back door and loaded a box into the van.

These poor women showed up to do their jobs. Now they're staring down the barrel of a gun and might not make it home that night. He couldn't help but think of the woman from earlier. When he took a picture with her son, she headed off to work wearing a uniform similar to that one.

He pressed his forehead against the cold bricks of the building. The wall nudged his fedora off his head, sending it tumbling to the ground in slow motion. He reached for it, but as he did, his fake glasses slipped from his face and clattered to the pavement.

He froze and listened. He hoped the idling engine of the van and the distance between him and the gunmen were enough that they heard nothing.

As he listened, no footsteps approached. The women murmured to each other and begged for their lives in Spanish. Peter caught a few words he learned to better communicate with tourists from Mexico. They have families. They're both mothers and they beg for their lives. The gunman tells them to shut up or he'll kill them.

They must not have heard his glasses fall. Peter scooped them up and his hat. He stuffed the glasses into his pocket and put the hat back on his head. He peeked around the corner again. The second assailant carried another box from inside and loaded it into the van.

Peter stepped back and walked a few steps away. His hands trembled as he dialed the police. The emergency operator answered. Peter did his best to whisper but his voice trembled as much as his hands.

"Hello, I'm witnessing a robbery right now," Peter said before the 911 operator finishes greeting him. "They have a gun and two hostages. I'm on Seventh Street between some buildings. I was walking home. Between the bank and Dynamic Precision. I don't know. They're loading boxes into a van. License plate? I didn't catch it. I can go back."

A scream pierces the night and rips Peter's attention away from his phone. He shoves the phone into his pocket and rushes back to the alley. He peeks around the corner again. One woman is sitting in the middle of the alley with her hands in front of her face. The gunman waved the gun at her, pointing to the street, where Peter watches.

"—do you think you're doing?" The gunman says. "You should have told me there was someone else inside. I could have shot him!"

Peter's heart dropped, and blood drained from his face. He looked down the alley and saw the little boy from earlier. A gunman dragged him out and threw him to the ground by his mother.

"It is them," Peter whispers to himself.

Peter heard a small mechanical voice, but he ignored the 911 operator trying to get his attention from his pocket. Guardian Man would do something. Peter was a hypocrite. He was so concerned about someone seeing Guardian Man smoking when he was talking to Doug, but what if someone saw Guardian Man being a coward? He hung up the call and stepped into the alley.

In his mind, he knew it was the right thing to do. Stupid, but morally just. He couldn't stand by and do nothing. She was a janitor with a kid who couldn't afford for someone to take care of her boy. Or couldn't trust anyone enough. Peter didn't know which would have been worse, but it didn't matter. She came to clean an office building to put food on the table. He wouldn't be able to live with himself if something happened, and he did nothing.

Besides, he wasn't "Peter." He was Peter Powers, mild mannered reporter, amateur underground fighter and secret superhero Guardian Man.

"Stop!" Peter shouted.

The words flew out of his mouth on instinct. Guardian Man's confidence was his confidence. In his mind, at that moment, Peter Price was Peter Powers. He was the embodiment of good and just. The hero of San Francisco, taking a trip to San Jose to stop the murder of an innocent civilian. He was indestructible and all-powerful.

He was a guardian.

"Hey! Get out of here," the gunman shouted, pointing his gun at Peter.

"Fear not," Peter continued, launching into his skit. "For I am not the man you assume me to be. I am a hero, a true guardian. I will protect the lovely people gracing the streets of San Jose."

Peter ripped open the magnetic buttons on his shirt and revealed the giant "G." The long purple cape cascaded down Peter's back in ripples. The fabric caught the low light of an explosion of fireworks in the sky. It fluttered down behind Peter's ankles and danced as it bounced, settling into graceful waves. By then, he was in full costume, his glasses and tear away clothes in a pile, off to the side.

"Let the innocent people leave," Peter said. "Your quarrel is now with me."

He placed his fists on his hips and took up the signature pose of Guardian Man, with his chest puffed out, belly sucked in, and a smile on his face.

"What is this? Did you escape the mental hospital?" the gunman says.

The gunman's attention is on Peter, his gun aimed. The second person is inside the building.

"Your gun is useless against me," Peter said, taking a step toward the bad guy with each word, and with each step, his confidence grew. "Any bullet you fire will fall to the ground. Any fist you throw will shatter against me. Anything you throw at me, I can dodge faster than the speed of light. I am a true guardian in all ways."

Peter saw the sweat on the gunman's brow and the fear in his eyes.

"Who do you work for?" Peter asks. "Dr. Corrupto? I didn't realize he was still recruiting henchmen. Didn't he learn his lesson last time? Cheap labor is so last year."

"Don't step any closer. I swear, crazy or not, I'll blow your fucking head off."

"There's a child present," Peter said. "Language like that is so foul. You must lack an education. No wonder you've fallen for Dr. Corrupto's henchmen ads. Your human weapons are no match for the power of Guardian Man. I know you don't want to hurt anyone or get hurt. Put the gun down and we can all have a happy life."

With the gunman's attention on Peter, he didn't notice the hostages sneaking away to safety. Peter kept talking, aware of their escape. Knowing they were safe made his chest swell with pride. He was a true guardian. A hero.

He grabbed the gunman and flew into the air so high the air grew thin. The gunman gasped for air and eked out an apology.

"I'm sorry, Guardian Man," the gunman said.

"Forgiveness is my strongest power, citizen," Guardian Man said, his voice soft and nurturing. "You are forgiven."

Guardian Man flew back to the ground, where the gunman gasped for air. Guardian Man threw him into the van. Cartoon birds circled above his head.

"I forgive you, but the law is not so forgiving," Guardian Man said.

Guardian Man dusted his hands off and closed the back door to the building. Blue and red lights flashed, and a siren wailed, getting louder with every second until it found the right alley and lit up Guardian Man in red and blue.

"Guardian Man?" an officer asked. "Is it really you? You're far from the city."

"It is, Officer," Guardian Man said, leaning against the alley wall. "And fear not, I've thwarted evil. I saved the hostages and the day.

Guardian Man rested his head, cocking it back against the cold brick of the wall. His breathing grew heavy. He trembled, pulling his hand in front of his eyes, and seeing the blood seeping through the cracks of his fingers. His head rolled. Something hard pressed against the back of it. It wasn't a brick wall he was leaning against; it was the ground of the alley.

The smell of the dumpster and the exhaust of a car reached his nose. He looked up and saw the scared face of the gunman. He stuffed the smoking gun into his waistband. His associate ran out from the building and leaned over Guardian Man.

"What the fuck did you do?" The second henchman said.

"I don't know. I don't know. Let's get out of here before the cops show up."

They clambered into the car and the tires of the van screeched as it sped out of the alley.

Peter looked down and saw the blood seeping across the "G" on his chest. He gasped for air and coughed. Blood spewed from his mouth and peppered his face. He couldn't swallow, could no longer breathe, instead he choked with every attempt. He wanted to vomit, but couldn't. His arms and legs went numb.

Peter's eyes fell shut, but he tried to force them open as he struggled to understand what was happening.

"No," he grumbled to himself. "I stopped them. I foiled them, right? Right?"

But the alley was empty, the night was black. No one heard his last words. The women and the child were gone. Safe somewhere. He smiled. A tear rolled down his face, then his eyes went blank, staring up at the sky. Stars twinkled in the distance. His chest went still. His heart stopped. Blood pooled around him in the empty alley.

In the distance, over the water of the bay, fireworks exploded. Bright colors filled the sky as the city celebrated.

| 9 |

VOODOO

The doll was adorable, with an uncanny likeness to her sister. She grabbed the pins and stuck them into the doll's eyes, smiling as her sister screamed in the next room.

| 10 |

I'M WATCHING YOU

Ariana's murder took place on a crisp autumn night. A breeze rolled through the city, wound through the skyscrapers and swooped down. It shoved aside pieces of litter and crawled along the sidewalk where it found her. It swirled around her in an icy embrace. She pulled her jacket tight.

Her footsteps were thunder in the quiet night. It was normal for the city to be quiet in that hidden hour, nuzzled between too late and too early.

A chill crept up her spine. At night, beyond the dark, anything can lie in wait. Deviants. Monsters. Murderers. Her mind raced through every possibility as she marched home. She read the graffiti clinging to the walls of the buildings to stop her mind from wandering. The smell of fresh paint stung her nostrils as she passed the painted words, *I'm watching you.*

She hated that her roommate left her car in their only parking spot. Gone for six weeks on a study abroad program. During the week, it was easy to find parking within a few blocks. On weekends she had to park a 17-minute walk away at least.

Late shifts were hard, but tending the bar on a busy weekend left her with enough to cover expenses. Books, tuition, food, rent. She glanced back over her shoulder.

A crumpled napkin bounced along the road, carried on a gust of soft, whispering wind. Nothing more. Not that night. She kept walking.

For the past few nights, Ariana swore someone followed her. She heard noises. Footsteps. Every time she looked back, there was nothing.

"You know how you stop at a red light and you look at the driver in the car next to you?" Ariana asked earlier that night.

"Yeah," her coworker said. His name was Reese, but everyone called him Peanut.

"At the same time, they look back at you like they knew you were looking at them? It feels like that," Ariana said. She lifted a stool and put it upside down on the table as Peanut mopped the floor beneath it. "Like someone is watching me and I get this weird feeling and look over. Then, when I look, there's nothing there, or it's too dark to see."

"That's creepy," Peanut said.

His flat voice did little to hide his disinterest. Ariana didn't notice. She kept talking, much to Peanut's dismay, but not to his surprise. He didn't have any real advice to offer. He went through the motions of the conversation as they closed for the night. If it wasn't one thing with Ariana, it was another. He shrugged and suggested buying pepper spray or a pocket knife. She agreed but knew she never would. Doing so would feel like an admission that some-one was following her. There was still a chance it was all in her head. She didn't think she was the type of person people stalk.

He didn't care what she decided and walked away before the conversation ended. He left her talking to herself for a few seconds before she realized she was alone.

That night, the odd feeling she had was gone. There were no strange sounds, no one hiding. Not that she felt, anyway. In her head, she debated if it was scarier to feel eyes on her or to feel none. If they weren't watching from the dark, where else might they be?

In the distance, her apartment waited for her. Almost home. She slid her keys through her fingers and made a fist. She knew it wouldn't provide much real protection, but it was enough to put her at ease as she reached the door. The landscapers made a nice effort of creating places for creeps to hide. There was a small cluster of thick bushes, a row of hedges, and a few large redwoods from when the city was a small town.

She slid the key into the lock and threw a last glance over her shoulder. Nothing. Ariana stepped inside. The security door slammed shut and echoed through the empty apart-ment lobby.

The elevator was quiet. There was a chemical smell that stung her nostrils. Spray paint? She pulled out her phone and clicked away.

"Still awake?" Ariana texted.

Her phone chimed back when she got off the elevator.

"Yeah. You home?" Valerie texted back.

They met two semesters ago and became quick friends. Ariana did all the talking. She wondered if Valerie was using her to get a good grade or if they were actually friends. Either way, she was happy to have someone to text at the end of the night. Valerie didn't seem to mind.

Ariana unlocked her apartment and slid through the door. The deadbolt clicked into place; she tugged the door to double-check the lock. She let out a sigh of relief.

Home.

Safe.

Still facing the door, she texted her friend back. Valerie was kind enough to stay up late to make sure Ariana got home. She didn't want to leave her waiting a moment longer.

"Home now. Thanks for staying up," Ariana texted.

"No problem. Everything good?" Valerie asked.

"Yup! I'm home safe. Maybe it was all in my head."

Something slipped out from the shadows and approached Ariana. Beyond the blue glow of her phone, she didn't notice.

"That's good. Better safe than sorry. Glad you're home. Gonna sleep now. Goodnight."

"Thank you again! Goodnight."

She slid the phone into her pocket and turned around. Her blood froze as she stared into the eyes of a stranger.

"Oh no," Ariana squealed. It was all she could muster before his hand clutched her mouth and stifled a scream.

He forced her back. Her head smacked against the door. Bright spots filled her vision. She pulled her phone from her pocket, but it tumbled out of her grasp and clattered on the floor. She tried to pry the hand from her mouth, but it was too strong. His other arm pressed across her chest, pinning her to the door. The dark figure towered over her. His smell stung her nostrils. Spray paint.

"I wish I could say this would be painless," the man said, his voice deep and garbled. "But I'd be lying. This will hurt. It will hurt a lot. It will be so beautiful."

He stretched out the word "beautiful" as his arm pulled away from her chest. He fiddled with something around his waist.

Moonlight poured through the window. Something shimmered. It moved too fast for her to see. A sharp pain struck in her gut. She tried to scream, but the hand still silenced her. She looked down and saw the knife plunge into her again.

Ariana slid to the floor. She flailed her arms, desperate to grab anything. Something soft fell into her grasp. She pulled. The unfamiliar face of her attacker appeared as the mask slid from his face. His blue eyes stared into hers.

She couldn't scream. She couldn't fight. All she felt was pain as the knife plunged into her again and again. Pressure built up inside her, pressing against her insides. She coughed into his hand and blood dribbled through his fingers. Her eyes rolled around the room, unable to focus.

Ariana fell to the floor. The attacker moved his hand from her mouth and wiped the blood on her jacket. Her scream came out as nothing more than a whimper.

Her hands were sticky. She smelled metal. She coughed a spray of blood across the floor in front of her.

She knew she was going to die. She would never walk home at night again. Never earn her degree or see where her path would have taken her. Regrets and wishes flooded her mind. She pictured her mother's face, the last hug she gave her father before he died. Her brother's smile.

It all ended there on the dirty floor of a two-bedroom apartment she struggled to afford. Blood dripped from her hands like all her dreams slipping through her fingers. She whimpered, then let out her last breath. Her body went still and cold. Her eyes stared at the ceiling as the killer stepped over her.

A week later, an article told the story of a bloody crime scene and a woman found dead in her apartment. Another tenant found her body. An unmistakable smell to the veteran two doors down. Police had no leads and asked the public to offer any information.

As she read the article on her phone, Valerie felt the nosy gaze of a passenger seated beside her on the train. From the corner of her eye, she saw a curious woman with a chubby toddler on her lap. Valerie smiled at the woman. The woman blushed and readjusted in her seat to give Valerie space.

"*Lo siento,*" the woman said. "I didn't mean to be nosy."

"*Está bien,*" Valerie said. Her Spanish was fluent, but she spoke with an American accent.

"I heard it's some cult or something," the woman said in English. "Satan worshippers, you know?"

"I doubt it," Valerie said. "A woman murdered in her apartment? Nothing supernatural about it. That's life, no?"

"You know, my sister had this ex, right? After they broke up, she heard some noises one night, went outside. Found a dead chicken. They smeared its blood across the fence. That's some old-world voodoo shit my aunties used to do back in *México*."

Valerie flashed an insincere smile as the PA crackled. The operator spat muffled nonsense over the intercom.

"This is my stop," Valerie said, halfway to the door by the time she finished talking.

The lady turned her attention back to her daughter, who stirred from a light nap. She sat her down in the seat Valerie left empty. The crowd pushed forward as the train neared the next stop. Through the chitter chatter of the other passengers, Valerie heard the woman rambling on about the article, mumbling something about *el diablo*.

They didn't name the victim in the article. Valerie hadn't heard from Ariana for a few days, not since that same night she texted her to make sure she got home safe. The article said the woman died that same night. She hadn't been in class since then either. Sand pumped through Valerie's heavy heart as she imagined the worst.

The two weren't that close, but Valerie enjoyed having someone to talk to since her breakup with Victor. She would have gone to Ariana's apartment to check on her, but she didn't know where she lived and she didn't have a car.

The bright lights inside the train cast a strong reflection in the window against the dark night on the outside. Valerie's reflection stared back at her. She did her best to look anywhere but into her own eyes.

The doors opened with a hiss, and the night air swirled into the train car. Rude passengers shoved their way in, boarding before waiting their turn. Valerie rolled her eyes and did her part to push through. She sucked in the fresh air of the outdoors, happy to escape the stale, recycled air of the train, until the stench of urine and cigarette smoke reminded her how disgusting the city could be.

Headphones clung to her ears. She stuck her thumbs into the shoulder straps of her backpack. All she wanted was a microwaved burrito and to get into bed and watch awful movies.

She crossed the park on her usual route, then through a parking lot to avoid a homeless encampment. The most unsettling part of her walk home was through a dark bike tunnel that went under an overpass. It was the quickest way home and the only route that avoided the crack den with regular police raids.

Valerie approached the edge of the bike tunnel, staring into the abyss. During the day, it seemed harmless enough and so much shorter than it seemed at night. Grass grew through the cracked ground. An exposed pipe spilled out a green residue along the wall by the entrance. The entire tunnel smelled like piss. Dim lights usually kept the tunnel lit, but that night only one light shone at the center of the tunnel. It flickered and hummed, casting deeper darkness around each tunnel entrance. The opposite end was too dark to see from where Valerie stood.

She took off her headphones and stepped into the tunnel.

Her footsteps echoed as she hurried through. A dim streetlamp across the street from the tunnel guided her. It grew brighter and more clear as she neared the exit. She kept her eyes focused on that light, then she froze. Something crossed the tunnel exit, blocking out the light for a moment before disappearing.

It was too far to see in the dark. Her heart sank and her hands trembled as she raised her phone and flicked on the flashlight. There was nothing there. Not that she could see.

She could turn back, but there was nowhere else to go, and home was a quick sprint away from the tunnel. She fumbled her keys out of her backpack. They fell to the ground, shattering the silence of the night. If someone didn't know she was there before, the keys gave her away. Valerie scooped them up and stepped forward, fingers wrapped around her pepper spray keychain.

Nearing the end of the tunnel, her heart smashed against her chest. A few steps away, there could be a madman waiting. If someone jumped out at her, she'd have to run for all her worth and not stop until she made it to her apartment. She stepped out of the tunnel and took in her surroundings.

Nothing.

A cool breeze, a bright moon, an empty park bench. Valerie sighed in relief. There was no one around that she could see, but she didn't want to wait for someone to pop out of the bushes. She hurried away from the tunnel and into the protection of the lights outside her apartment.

It stood three stories high. Filled with low-income families and college kids who couldn't afford dorms. Built in the 60s, renovated in the 80s, not touched since. Valerie suspected paper clips and bubble gum held it all together. Her own apartment was on the first floor.

As she got closer to her building, her skin crawled. A strange feeling crept across her chest and wrapped around her throat. She walked faster, looking over her shoulder but not seeing anything in the darkness behind her.

She could see the light shining through the security door of her apartment. The light was always on, and she had never been more thankful. The locks clicked open as her key fob chirped, and she stepped inside. She peered through the glass as the locks clicked into place.

A car pulled in and crossed to the guest parking. The headlights of the car swept over the apartment complex. They illuminated a dark figure standing in bushes across the parking lot. The headlights moved away as the car found a place to park.

Valerie took a deep breath. She stared at where the figure waited in the darkness, hoping to see it move. She'd be happy to know it was nothing, but if it was someone following her, she wanted to know who or why or where they were. Another car pulled into the parking lot. Valerie stared at the bushes. As the headlights swept across the building, it landed there again. This time there was no dark figure, nor anything that might be mistaken for a person.

Gone.

As she got ready for the night, she checked the doors and windows. Then she double-checked them and checked them a third time.

In the last moments, before dozing off for a much-needed night's sleep, she checked Victor's social media. It was a bad idea, but she needed to know it wasn't him in the bushes. She didn't know what to expect. Even if it was him, he wouldn't post a selfie of him stalking her. What Valerie found hurt her more.

He posted a picture of himself on a date with another woman. He tagged the location. They were away on a trip together and were nowhere near Valerie's apartment. He tagged the woman in the picture. The woman commented with a heart. He replied a few seconds ago with a blushing smiley face. Internet sleuthing convinced Valerie it was all real. She didn't envy the woman; she felt cold. Forgotten already by a man she wished she never knew. She spent hours dissecting the life of her replacement, reading anything and everything she could find on her, until she fell asleep, all but forgetting the man in the bushes.

The next night, Valerie dreaded the walk home. Rideshares were too expensive. Owning a car was out of the question. She already worked full time and struggled to keep herself afloat in such an expensive city.

There was no pedestrian access on the road. The bus didn't go near her apartment building. Her only choice was to walk home and stay vigilant. She kept her pepper spray handy. She hoped it was a stranger in the night who would have forgotten about her by the time the sun rose. As soon as she approached the dark bike tunnel, she knew she was wrong.

Valerie felt eyes on her. She looked around and quickened her pace. The eyes studied her from somewhere in the dark. She couldn't tell from where they watched, but knew they watched. There were too many shadows for a stranger to use as a hiding spot. Too many parked cars along the streets. In any of them, her watcher could peek through the window, waiting for his moment.

Ariana still hadn't replied to any of Valerie's texts and the news offered no updates on the woman found stabbed. Another forgotten victim. Valerie knew in her heart that it was Ariana. She mentioned someone might be following her. Valerie regretted not paying closer attention. Ariana said a lot of things about a lot of things. It was too easy to not listen to what she said.

She took a deep breath and entered the tunnel. Her phone glowed in the darkness with 9-1-1 dialed and ready to call. Graffiti mocked her as she passed with generic threats and boasts. One phrase caught her eye. The words scrawled across the painting made her hands go numb. The potent smell of the fresh paint stung her nostrils.

I'm watching you.

A sweat broke out beneath her shirt as she picked up her pace and made her way out of the tunnel. She glanced back and saw something move in the darkness. Her heart pumped away and before she knew it, her feet pounded on the pavement. Her legs moved faster than she thought possible. Fire erupted in her lungs, and her backpack felt heavier than ever. She debated on throwing it to the ground to stop it from slowing her down, but knew it wasn't an option. She had homework, half-finished projects, and a beaten up laptop inside.

The warmth of her apartment had never been so welcome. She pulled back the edge of her curtain and peered out the window into the parking lot. The bushes where she saw the figure the night before were empty. She sighed in relief but stayed vigilant, scanning the parking for anything out of place. She held her breath as if whoever might be watching could hear her heavy breathing.

As the curtain fell back in place, she thought she saw something at that last moment. She peeked back out, careful not to let a potential spectator see her. Her breath cast fog on the window. She reached one of her slender fingers out and wiped the fog. Across the street from her apartment, the streetlamp outside the tunnel lit the sidewalk. A dark figure stepped into the center. From what she could see, he wore all black. A long jacket. Dark pants. Something obscured his face. It was hard to tell where he began and the surrounding shadows ended.

She squinted to see better. The figure was a man. Tall. His head turned on a swivel. There was no way he could see her from so far away, but she knew he looked right at her looking at him. His eyes drank her in and filled her with dread. Stumbling away from the window, she grabbed her phone. She swiped open the camera and aimed it out the window to take a picture for the police report.

He was gone.

She looked around to see if he was moving toward the apartment. She checked the bushes again. The street. The sidewalk. Nothing. No one. Not that she could see, anyway. She triple-checked the lock on the door and on all the windows. She was safe in her home, though she couldn't help but feel more vulnerable than ever.

She took a day off and stopped at the police station. An annoyed peace officer took notes as she explained what she had been going through. He checked his phone halfway through her story before he asked what proof she had.

"Proof?" Valerie said. "I have nothing, I'm not sure what you—"

"I don't see what we can do," the officer said, not looking up. "You have no evidence. There have been no threats. It could be a homeless person hanging around. You're getting in your own head."

"No," Valerie said. "There's someone following me. I know it. I've seen them watching me from outside my apartment."

"How do you know he was watching you?"

"He was across the street, but I knew he was—"

"Best we can do, an officer drives by every so often."

"Can they give me a ride? I get off at—"

"We're police officers, not rideshares. If you need a ride, ask a friend, use an app."

Waste of time. She had no friends. All her friends were Victor's, and she hadn't heard from any of them since the breakup. Useless.

That night, an odd sound in the living room ripped Valerie from a light sleep. She jumped out of bed and grabbed her phone. Tip-toeing to her bedroom door, she cracked it open and looked down the hall to the living room. She recognized the sound right away. The doorknob into her apartment made a creaking sound when she turned it. That night, she was thankful for the landlord's procrastination about fixing it.

The sounds stopped. For a moment, she wondered if the stranger made his way into the apartment or gave up and left.

Valerie crept down the hallway, illuminated by a single nightlight doing its best to fend off the darkness. Her eyes swept the living room. From what she could see, nothing seemed out of place, and her apartment was too small to afford many hiding spots. The door grew larger as she stepped nearer. It towered over her. She stood still, waiting to hear it again. Pieces of metal rubbed against each other. The doorknob twitched but didn't turn; the lock doing its job. It held on for dear life. Her icy hands trembled. At least it meant the stranger was outside the door and not inside the apartment. Not yet anyway.

She dialed 9-1-1 on her phone and poised her thumb over the call button. She leaned in and put her eye to the peephole. On the other side, an eye looked back. An eye she didn't recognize. Her hand flew to her mouth to stifle a scream.

She stumbled back, then turned and ran toward her bedroom. She slammed the door shut and locked it behind her. Valerie climbed into bed, hand still stifling her scream. Her eyes watered. Her body went numb. She moved her hand away and gasped for breath. Her chest heaved as she panted and cleared her mind. She looked over at a burnt-out candle on the nightstand. She remembered the woman on the bus and what she said about occultists and chicken blood.

A call to the police would be easy, but how would they even find him? Would they be any help or a waste of time again? Her finger still hovered over the dial button. She already spoke to the police. They were useless. There was a better way, a way that would put an end to it forever.

She deleted the dialed 9-1-1 and opened her contacts. In the darkness, her face bathed in light, Victor's number stared at her. There was no other option. Her fingers flew across her keyboard but froze at the sound of a light tap on her window.

Tap, tap.

She looked at the closed curtain, glad she checked the locks.

Tap, tap, tap.

Her heart raced. She imagined what might wait on the other side of the glass. With no luck at the door, he must have tried the window. The image of a deranged face, covered in madness, shot through her mind.

Tap, tap, slam!

The window rattled as something slammed into the outside of the window. She heard footsteps stomp off into the distance. Moments passed. She strained her ears for any other sound. It was hard to hear over the thundering of her own heart.

She finished her text and sent it off to Victor.

She locked herself in the bathroom, curled into a ball, shivering in the cold tub. The bath mat she stole off the floor served as her blanket. It would be the last time she let fear chase her from the comfort of her own bed.

The next day, the train doors hissed, and Valerie stepped off. She took a minor detour from her usual route home. There was a small bar that had an open patio in the back. Music blared from inside and a small crowd shouted over each other. Part of her yearned to see him again. She wanted to take him home and spend the night ravishing each other like when they first started dating. The other part of her knew it would bring trouble back into her life. She had to be strong and in control, even if he begged.

She knew he'd be wearing his green button up. He thought it made his stomach look small and his arms big. A gentle finger tapped her shoulder. It took a moment for her to recognize Victor.

Her heart melted. Her eyes crawled up his body, drinking him in as she spoke. He looked better. Healthier. His face was more full. The bags that once hung from beneath his eyes were flat and colorful instead of heavy and dark.

The spiced aftershave brought her back to their late-night talks. He wasn't wearing the green button-up. Instead, he wore a solid gray henley with rolled-up long sleeves. He left the buttons open where his chest tattoo peeked at her. She offered a smile he didn't return.

"What do you need this for?" he asked, voice stern. No "hello." He held up a paper bag, the top folded down, sealing the bag and hiding the contents from any curious onlooker.

He avoided looking her in the eyes and instead let his pupils dance on something behind her.

"Have you been following me?" Valerie asked.

"Following you? No. Are you kidding me?" Victor said. He finally looked her in the eyes. "Did you use this to get me out here to play more of your mind games?"

"No, I swear. Can I have the bag?" Valerie asked, holding out her hand.

"Why would you ask if I was following you? Is someone following you?"

"I can handle it."

She reached out for the bag and let her hand brush against his. She felt his hand tremble and heard his breath escape his lungs. He took a small step back and pulled the bag away from her reach. He shook his head like a drunk sobering up for a dangerous drive home.

"With this?" Victor asked. "You know how dangerous this is?"

Valerie had little patience for another lecture. Still, her heart fluttered at the sound of his voice, even if it was harsh and stung with each syllable.

"I know how to use it. I've used it before."

"Right. Look who I'm talking to. You, of all people, know how dangerous this can be. If anything goes wrong, I don't want this to come back to me. I swear you're going to be the death of me one day. Why did I even come here?"

He turned away, but stopped and turned back, then paced in front of her. She followed with her eyes, unblinking. Patience wore thin as the night grew dark.

"Are you going to give it to me or not?" Valerie asked.

"Here."

Victor shoved the bag into Valerie's arms a little too hard. She stumbled back half a pace. He stepped in close, his face inches away. His hand brushed against hers and they both blushed. He cleared his throat. His voice deflated.

"After this, lose my number. I want nothing to do with you. Understand? I moved on."

"Okay," Valerie said, and nothing else.

Her eyes watered, but she blinked the tears away. The paper bag was heavier than she remembered. They studied each other's faces. His shoulders relaxed. His tattooed hand scratched his eyebrow as he searched for something to say.

"Look," he said. "I don't want you to get hurt or anything. Just because we didn't work out or whatever, doesn't mean I hate you."

"I know."

"Is someone hurting you?" Victor asked. His voice was sincere. Concerned.

"Someone has been following me. I think. I mean, I know someone has. When I walk home at night. Alone."

"You need a ride? Why don't you let me drop you off?"

"No," Valerie said. "I'll be okay."

She bit her lip and hugged the paper bag in her arms, feeling the bumps and shape of what hid inside.

"Well, that's fine. Be careful, you know? Are you sure you don't need help to use it?"

"I have to go now."

"Okay. Bye, Valerie. Be careful."

Valerie turned away from him. She paused and looked back. She wished he wore that green button up.

"You look good. Take care," Valerie said. She walked off into the night, wondering if he watched her walk away and if she'd ever see him again.

With Victor behind her, Valerie needed to make haste to get home. Her meeting with him threw off her schedule. Whoever was watching might get angry.

She held the paper bag with a white knuckle grip and made her way along her usual route.

The tunnel entrance yawned a dark welcome. She'd be lying to herself if she said her heart didn't skip a beat or two as she stepped into the tunnel. The old words on the wall taunted her for the last time.

I'm watching you.

The paper bag grew heavy in her arms, and a smile crept across her face.

The apartment watched her as she crossed the parking lot. A car's headlights washed over her and guided her to the front door.

Once inside, she headed into her bedroom down the hall without stopping to take off her shoes or put down her purse. Had she bothered to triple-check the locks, she might not have missed the dark figure waiting in the shadows of her tiny living room.

Instead, the door remained unlocked, and the figure remained unnoticed. He crept across the room behind her. A gentle breeze brushed aside the curtains over the sink. Moonlight glinted off the shards of shattered glass in the sink.

Valerie left the door to her room cracked open, an invitation to her guest as she prepared. She assembled the pieces as needed and tossed the empty paper bag over her shoulder. Footsteps near the bedroom door told her she was no longer alone. The door creaked open, and the footsteps drew nearer. He even kicked the paper bag at her as he made his way over.

"I wish I could say this would be painless," he said. "But I'd be lying. This will hurt. It will hurt a lot."

Valerie paid no attention to him or the high-pitched squeal of his knife as he drew it from its sheath. Instead, she stayed on her knees, hunched over and fiddling with something in front of her. He leaned over and looked to see what had her so occupied that she ignored his threat. It didn't matter. He already missed his chance of escaping alive.

In front of Valerie, painted onto the floor, was a symbol. A pentagram, but with curved points that each split into horns. No. Not paint. Blood. In the center of the symbol was a human skull with intricate carvings etched onto the surface. A candle stood atop the skull, stuck to the forehead with melted wax. As the tiny flame flickered, it ate the candle. Melted wax dripped down the side and flowed through the skull's carvings.

She kept her eyes closed and whispered beneath her breath. Her soft voice made it hard to hear. The words were ancient, and She who needed to hear those words heard them clearly enough.

Behind the intruder, the nightlight in the living room dimmed and went dark. The doorway faded from a moonlit night to inescapable blackness. It was a darkness so deep nothing would ever escape, not a flicker of light or a scream.

From the darkness, a voice spoke. It bellowed and grumbled, shaking Valerie's skeleton with each word. Frames on the walls trembled and rattled. The words were ancient and only Valerie understood. Neither needed to understand the words to feel the dread that filled that room.

The intruder's face went pale. He spun around and stared into the dark void behind him. Valerie smiled and continued to chant the ancient words. The words she spoke were long forgotten by the living, but not forgotten to She who answered them.

The intruder turned back to Valerie. He had enough of her parlor tricks. He brought the knife over his head.

One of Her hands, decayed and green in hue, reached out from the deep dark and clutched his face, stifling his scream.

The darkness grew. It entered the room and swallowed the doorway and the wall and the ceiling.

More hands reached out and wrapped around the intruder. One wrapped around his own hand, in which he held the blade. Another reached out and grabbed his throat. Then came another and another and many more. Some hands burned where they touched him, others felt like ice. Some stung and others poked.

One hand, with gnarled talons on the end of each finger, grabbed his face. The forefinger pierced his eye, and the pinky latched onto his cheek. As it pulled on him, his skin ripped open and blood seeped out, dripping through the creature's fingers.

He was ready to scream, but the hand over his mouth muffled his cries for help. The knife fell from his grip and stuck into the hardwood. He fell to the ground, digging his nails into the wood as the hands pulled him toward the deep dark.

Valerie knew something terrible awaited him in the darkness, and she was glad to send him there. He would never hurt another young woman. He would make no one fear the dark.

The hands pulled him away into the darkness. The last sounds of his struggle went silent. She waited an extra moment to give Her and Her darkness time to leave. The walls and the door returned and the light in her living room once again lit the way.

She whispered in the ancient tongue and thanked Her and said Her name. It was a name long forgotten by Her original followers and known only by a few occultists. Valerie smiled again and leaned down. She inhaled, and with a sharp breath, blew out the candle.

| 11 |

BUTCHER

Finished with his deed, he cleaned off his knife and gazed upon his work. Her last words begged for him to leave her face alone for her funeral, but he decided instead to cut it off and take it with him.

| 12 |

THE BENELOFT HOTEL

A homeless man shuffled across the entrance of The Beneloft Hotel. He pushed his overflowing shopping cart, the squeaky wheel rattling. It called for the attention of the well-dressed guards who shooed him away.

The Beneloft Hotel was an edifice of timeless grandeur. Times have changed since the heyday of the Beaux Arts architecture in San Francisco. The luxury that led to its construction is still there, built into the foundation of the beautiful building, despite the city decaying around it.

Sleek windows glinted among the cream-colored stone. Intricate carvings and massive stone columns drew the eyes of tourists and historians alike.

People clad in designer clothes tossed keys for their six-figure cars. Valets, who struggled to afford a meal, snatched the keys from the air and hurried along. Lush greenery lined the walkway to the entrance, despite the bone-dry hills in the distance suffering from a year-long drought. Large doors yawned a wide welcome, held open by smiling, white-gloved doormen.

The inside of the hotel was no less grand. Marble floors stretched out underfoot, gleaming with a vibrant shine and speckled with glittering golden flakes. The soaring ceiling looked down with gilded moldings and crystal chandeliers that sparkled in the natural light which shone throughout the lobby.

A member of the staff greeted each guest with a warm smile, a gentle welcome, and a cinnamon tea with lemon. The hotel streamlined their check-ins because people with money had too much to do to deal with the tediousness of everyday life.

Even the air in The Beneloft Hotel was legendary, with a tantalizing blend of scents — citrus and fresh flowers.

Thick carpets lined the hallways with dark hues of burgundy and deep purple inspired by the violet of an amethyst. Ornate sconces lit the hallways, matching the painted gold trim of the molding. At the end of the hall on the highest floor awaited a door so thick that a scream couldn't escape, offering unfounded privacy to the many affluent guests who called that room home for a night or a month.

Entering the penthouse suites continued the journey of unparalleled luxury. Panoramic windows offered breathtaking views of the Golden Gate Bridge and Alcatraz Island. At night, the city came alive with the flickering of a million tiny lights.

The bed was a massive California King with thick down blankets and overstuffed down pillows. Jonathan Carmichael sat on the bed with his head buried in his hands. He was a man who had everything. He built an empire and amassed a fortune. A night at The Beneloft Hotel was nothing to him and in a few years, he could build a luxury hotel of his own without batting an eye if things continue as they had been going for decades. A slight hiccup to those dreams lay sprawled across the floor of that penthouse suite.

The pure white shag of the carpet bore drops of a dark crimson that matted the shag. At the center of the carpet, the pale blue eyes of a dead whore stared up at the chandelier. Jonathan whispered pleas of forgiveness, begging the empty room to make it all go away. As he peeked between his fingers, he knew it was real. Her chest neither rose nor fell, just lay still. His face burned. Everything he had worked so hard for was about to be washed away in a river of her tainted blood. Flashes of their time together played back in his mind as if it were a portal to another world where he could choose a time to go back to and make everything alright. He remembered seeing her on the street, beautiful and nearly bare, an opportunity he couldn't pass up. She smiled at him. Cash and loneliness overruled his better judgment.

It didn't take long for the whore to be naked on top of him, showing him the love that had been so absent from his life. Women weren't scarce, but a woman with nothing to say was much preferred for him and it was all he wanted that night. His career has been skyward for as long as he could remember and an exploratory committee had green-lit a bid for his political ambitions.

He was untouchable.

So he got rough. His wife's words played back in his head, calling him name after name, insult over insult. As he fucked the whore in that opulent hotel room, he wrapped his hands around her throat and squeezed. At first, it was a gentle, playful fun that toyed with the thought of it turning into something more. Then he pressed down harder and felt her body tighten. His face grew hot, and he squeezed tighter until her face turned blue. She slapped and pulled and scratched at him. He balled a fist with his other hand and laid into her until she stopped fighting back. Blood dripped off his knuckles and from her nose. Broken teeth clattered to the tile on the floor between the bed and the shag carpet. By the time his nerves had calmed, she was dead. He tossed her off the bed with a kick from his heavy leg. She rolled across the floor and came to a halt in the center of the room.

He was the most powerful man in the world for only a moment until he realized he was the most vulnerable man in the world. If anyone heard anything or walked through that door, he'd lose it all. It would destroy his political ambitions, bring his company crashing to the ground, and sweep away his fortune. All because of a night of passion, an overgrown ego, and a dead whore no one would care about.

No. He built his empire from nothing and the last thing he would do was let a dead whore upend everything for him. He had to get rid of her. He knew little about that world, the world in which a man gets rid of a body, but he knew there had to be a way.

He walked over to his suitcase and dug through it to find the right shirt, something easy to move in that he wouldn't mind ditching if he had to. As he dug through the suitcase, he stepped back and took in the size and shape of it, then turned back to the girl.

He flipped the suitcase over and dumped the clothes across the bed, then threw the suitcase on the floor.

Her corpse was heavy. A younger version of him would have had no issue lifting her. The days sitting behind desks, taking in meetings with sugary foods, and heavy dinners with fat cats of tech, had all taken their toll on his health.

But what was the point of all this success if he still cowered at the sharp tongue of his wife? He still caved in at every word shouted by his spoiled children. Between them and the shareholders and the board of directors, the journalists and the protestors, he had little control over anything. He had all the power in the world, yet none.

The fragile whore's little neck was so warm in his hand. It was no wonder to him why he squeezed so tight. He looked into her eyes and saw the younger woman his wife had once been. Every frustration and every demon bubbled to the surface as he squeezed tighter. Then, as her eyes went dull, those demons faded away. Relief swept over him. He wanted to continue lying to himself, to act like it was an accident, that things got away from him.

He looked into her dead eyes and saw his younger wife once again. Before the kids, before the arguing, before the damage of time had turned her from something he loved into someone he despised. He knew he did what he did with some intention. Even if he buried it beneath the heat of passion.

He rolled the girl into the suitcase, then sat down against the bed to catch his breath. The young whore's limbs dangled over the edges of the suitcase. Her head peered over the zipper and stared at him.

"I'm not sorry," he said, staring back into her cold, pale stare. "I didn't plan for this. No. I can't say that I did. But I won't let you destroy everything I've built. Do you know who I am? I am Jonathon Carmichael. If your family knew you were with me...You know, I guess I have little to say. I feel like I should say something like you need me to say something. But there's nothing to say. I didn't plan for this. All I wanted was one night, one night to not feel so unimportant. I know I'm one of the most important men in the world, and yet...Anyway, this isn't personal. I hope you understand that. Not that it matters. I've bought and destroyed people with larger dreams than you ever could have even fathomed. You are nothing to me."

His own last words echoed through his head as he stared back at the girl. He knew a place in the woods, outside the city. No one went into that area. He had gone there with a girl he knew in college and they explored each other's bodies throughout the night, undisturbed. It would be an undeniable synchronicity. The first girl he made love to, and the old whore he strangled. There was poetry in there somewhere, but he couldn't quite grasp it. He was never much of a creative person.

Grunting as he stood, he made his way back to the suitcase and pushed her head down into it, its fabric stretched taut at the seams. His brow furrowed in concentration as he wrestled with her corpse. He studied her body as he manipulated her to make her fit. Each scar told a story, and each scratch was a memory. Every little tattoo hidden away told of her life, including one that he discovered covered with makeup. Why had she covered that single tattoo but not the others? They were initials, small and common. Did she hide them from her clients, or herself? Her life had been long-lived and harsh, and now her story is an old book, collecting dust and long forgotten.

As he forced the suitcase's zipper, he felt the weight of an impossible choice. He pushed and prodded, gritting his teeth in frustration. The corpse resisted, digging into the suitcase's lining. Each shove sent a fresh wave of panic through him. The suitcase remained ajar, taunting him with the impossibility of fitting her life into such a mundane thing. No matter how he moved her or how he tried to make her fit, her eyes would always be there, looking at him, and they would always be there every time he closed his own.

Finally, in a moment of desperation, he sat back on his heels, breathless. He knew what he had to do. With trembling hands, he grasped her forearm and raised it to eye level, studying the intricacies. Then, with a heavy resolve, he positioned it at an angle against the suitcase's edge, pressing down until the first crack echoed in the room's silence. Pain radiated through him as he heard it. Each subsequent break felt like a jagged shard piercing his chest, but he forced himself to continue. He bit his lip, blinking back the sting of tears as he finally fit the remnants of his beloved whore into the suitcase. He pulled the zipper, which danced around the suitcase without so much as a tug or a pause.

It was done. He changed into new clothes and left his sweaty outfit on the floor of his bathroom. Making his way to the door, he grabbed his keys. He peered out, ensuring the hallways were clear, and no sounds came from the adjacent rooms. By the time he could close the suitcase, most of the night had gone, and he was well into the early hours of the morning. If he had any luck left, he would only need to speak to the valet to retrieve his car.

Though it was on wheels, the suitcase was heavier than expected. It reminded him of when he retrieved his mother's ashes from the mortuary. They reduced her entire body to ash and placed it inside a tiny box no larger than something he would bring her with a pair of designer shoes. It was a small box, but heavier than expected.

As he realized earlier, he wasn't the young man he once was, and the hours of contorting her body to fit into the suitcase had taken a toll on him. He was weary. Heavy bags hung under his dry eyes. He trudged along the hallway and toward the elevator. The lavishness of the hotel suddenly appeared dull. The torture had muted the vibrancy in his mind. As he reached for the elevator button, he heard the bell ring. The door at the end of the bay of elevators opened to the sound of drunken voices and laughter. He turned the corner and went into the stairwell. Each step echoed down to the ground floor. Heaving the heavy suitcase down step by step grew tiresome. So he weighed his options and opted to turn back to the elevator and hope that no one else was awake. The drunken voices should be back in their rooms by that point. He turned and leaned over to heave the suitcase back up the step he had just gone down when his eyes caught something dark stained on the concrete step. A spot of blood.

His heart sank, and he felt his blood drain from his face. He turned back down toward the stairs to see if perhaps someone had spilled something else before him, but further down the steps beyond where he had walked, there was nothing. Behind him, there was a trail of dripped blood, smeared every few steps by the wheels of the suitcase.

"No," he muttered to himself. "No, no, no. No!"

He reached into his pocket and pulled out a kerchief and tried to wipe the blood on the step nearest him. As he let go of the suitcase, it toppled over and slid down the rest of the steps to the next landing where the zipper tore open and the dead body spilled out of the suitcase and lay flopped across the landing. Her broken limbs dangled about her body and her cold, empty eyes stared up at him once again.

He wondered what else could go wrong, then a realization hit, and he turned to the wall. His eyes scaled up into the corner to the blinking red light on a surveillance camera.

He looked back at the body, up at the camera, then down to the bloody smears behind him. He knew that the blood must lead a trail right back to his room. Given his situation, there was no way it wouldn't. Everything he had worked so hard for had just fallen out of that suitcase. There wasn't enough money in the world to clean this up.

A door above him opened, and two large men in suits stepped toward him.

"Mr. Carmichael," one man said. "Please return to your room."

He turned and looked down the stairs and saw another two men standing there. One of them motioned for him to follow the men up the stairs, and the other man knelt and inspected the dead body.

"Now, please, Mr. Carmichael," the man upstairs said again.

He nodded and made his way up the stairs. As he hung his head and walked, he watched the little spots of blood that had dripped into the carpet lead the way back to his room, as he suspected.

"Sit," said the man in the suit.

He did as he was told and sat with his head buried in his hands. Tears streamed down his face and dripped through his fingers.

After some time, the door opened again, and he heard the man in the suit greet someone. He assumed it was a police officer, but when he looked up, it was an unassuming man in a similar suit with a red triangle tucked into the pocket of his blazer.

"Hello, Mr. Carmichael. I'm the concierge for The Beneloft Hotel. You can call me Mr. Yung. I heard you had an incident in the stairwell."

"I'm so sorry," Jonathan said. "I didn't mean to..."

"Mr. Carmichael, I wish you would have exercised some discretion. You risked disturbing our other guests."

"What? A woman is dead and I...you're worried about bothering guests?"

"We deal with an affluent clientele. A clientele that finds issues with toeing the line with certain laws, and so we've become accustomed to people in your situation and have an option available."

"I'm sorry, what do you..."

"What I'm saying, Mr. Carmichael, is that we have a service you can use to help make this situation go away."

"Go away?"

"I need you to listen and understand. Time is of the essence. You're a smart man, you're quite accomplished. I need you to look at this like a business deal and keep your head in the game. What I'm offering you is a get-out-of-jail option that will make the girl go away, and keep your reputation and life intact. All it costs is $50,000 today."

Jonathan fell out of his trance. His head snapped over to the concierge, and he repeated the price back in shock.

"Ah, there you are. Once you put a price tag on a human life, people pay attention. Yes, if you would like to upgrade to our platinum special, it would be a fee of $50,000, followed by a secondary fee of $30,000 in three years to continue our support. After the second payment, you're free."

"$80,000? This is a shakedown."

"It's the cost of going home tonight and not going to jail."

"And where'd that number come from?"

"As I mentioned, time is of the essence, Mr. Carmichael. I've been here for some time and I know how this works. You can threaten us, but it would get you nowhere. We always get what's ours. The longer you wait, the more people will notice she's missing, and the more likely it is that someone will find the spots of blood in the hallway or the dead girl in the stairwell. If you sign now, we still have time to get ahead of this and clear everything up. The money isn't an issue for you. We checked. The morality of it isn't an issue for you. We checked that too. Please, sign the tablet."

"There's a form?"

"Everything needs a form, but don't worry. We leave out the specifics. As far as anyone knows, you broke an important sculpture and agreed to pay for it to be fixed. If you reconsider or refuse to pay, we can always send a copy of the surveillance video to you to review to see if you would like to continue with our support. We can send it to your home, where you live with Margaret Carmichael and little Anthony and Chelsea. Or we can send it to your workplace, or even your campaign office. Whatever is most convenient to you."

Jonathan nodded and reached out for the tablet, where he swiped his finger across and signed the agreement.

"So it's blackmail," he said, handing the tablet back.

The door opened and a team of people with suitcases came in.

"It's a mutually beneficial exercise in partnership, Mr. Carmichael. You get to go on and live your life with no worries of retribution or being caught for this. You don't need to worry about where to hide the body or if anyone would find the receipt you left in the front pocket of the suitcase. We don't have our business ruined by being the place where a rich executive strangled a coke-addled whore. There are stipulations, of course."

"Stipulations? We should have gone over that before I signed."

"It wouldn't have mattered, because you would have agreed either way. We know you picked her up on First Street and that she worked for a particular pimp we've had to pay off before. Part of your fee will go towards that. The rest covers the cleaning, disposal, the inconvenience to our other guests, and it pays for the discretion of our loyal staff. First, tell us everything she touched."

Jonathan pointed out a few things and the team disinfected and wiped those things down. Then they stripped the bed and replaced it with new sheets and blankets. Another took her belongings in a bag and carried them away. People hurried around him, dusting and wiping and cleaning. In the hallway, a steam cleaner hummed and sucked all the blood from the carpet.

The concierge took a seat and waited until everything was cleaned and the team was done, then he nodded goodbye and closed the door behind him. Jonathan stared at the closed door for a moment, still processing everything that had happened.

His phone buzzed, and he picked it up, checking the time before answering.

"Hey, honey."

"Jonathan, what was this withdrawal?"

"Oh, it's embarrassing. I bumped into this sculpture and they need to repair it. It was a whole thing."

"$50,000 for repairs? Are you kidding me? If I had a dollar for every time you did something so stupid, so clumsy, I could pay for those repairs myself."

He rubbed his temples and took a deep breath.

"It's fine. Don't worry about it. It's none of your business."

"$50,000 isn't my business? Who do you think you're talking to?"

"Hey, look, I'm exhausted. I think I'm going to be a little late coming home."

"How late?"

"I'm gonna stay another night."

| 13 |

SONG

Her beautiful voice floats on the wind, the words of her songs become enchanted commands. The hunters turn and do as the song says, raising their arms and taking aim at one another.

| 14 |

DARK ROAD

One day, a car cut us off at an intersection.

"Follow them," I demanded.

And Robbie did.

Like so many terrible things, it started as a game.

Cruising around Milpitas killed time when we were bored. We didn't go anywhere in particular. We drove wherever the road took us. Or rather, Robbie drove. I didn't have a car so it was always him driving and me sitting in the passenger seat fiddling with the music.

That night we were both in the mood that led to bad decisions. The car came out of nowhere when they cut us off. I didn't know why I wanted to follow them, but we had nothing else to do.

We kept our distance. When they turned, we turned. If they made it through a light, Robbie hit the gas and darted through the intersection too. Eventually, the car made it to their home, and we pulled to a stop across the street from their house. They didn't notice us. They walked inside without a glance over their shoulders. It was an older couple, though we were in our teens so older back then wasn't very old. The woman was pregnant, and the man rushed around the car to open the door for her.

We watched them go inside then waited outside their house, watching them move room to room. Lights flicked on and off, their shadows paced around the house. Eventually, the lights went out and everything was still. Cigarette smoke wafted through our car. The only light was the small blue screen of the car's radio accompanied by the gentle hum of music.

"Now what?" Robbie asked.

"They didn't even notice we were following them," I said.

As I said that, another car drove by. Robbie and I looked at each other and shared a sinister smile.

Robbie stepped on the gas pedal, and a new pursuit ensued. Last time we stayed hidden, trailing behind by a few cars, blending in. That time we stayed close. We didn't drive on their tail, but we stayed behind them and took every turn they took. As we made our way through the suburbs and they turned down specific streets on their way home, they caught on.

They signaled left.

We did too.

But they turned right.

We did too.

Robbie pressed the gas and flicked on the high beams. We were on their tail, an inch away from a collision. They sped up. We stayed on top of them until their car lurched to the right and they went down a needless loop that brought them out to the main road.

We did too.

I imagine they were scared by then. We did not know who was driving. It could have been a little old lady or young teenager out on her first drive alone. It could have been someone our age with a gun in their waistband, or someone who was tired and wanted to go home. We didn't know what we planned to do if they ever confronted us, probably speed off and disappear into the night, leaving them perplexed with a scary story to tell.

My heart pounded in my chest, and goosebumps grew across my arms. It was a rush. We didn't need to say a word. Robbie and I were of one mind. We both wanted to get closer, to intimidate them more and more, to see how far we could push them. How far would they go to escape a faceless stalker?

The car settled into a parking spot in front of a boba shop that was open late and hosted car meets in the parking lot. This meant lots of people late into the night.

We took this as a loss and decided instead to go inside and get a snack and boba for ourselves. We parked at the opposite end of the parking lot, letting our target escape.

In line for drinks, two young women stood in front of us. They danced in their spot, looking back over their shoulders, out the store's window. Gossip whispered between them, but as their nerves eased, their words got louder and I heard what they were saying.

"Do you see the car?" one of them asked.

"No, I don't know. It was so dark I didn't even see what it looked like."

They were much younger than us. Sixteen or seventeen. Their eyes were wide, their skin pale, and their hands trembled as they clicked around on their phones.

Robbie and I exchanged a look and held back a smile as he pretended to review the menu behind the counter.

"I should call my dad," one of them said.

"No, we aren't even supposed to be out. He thinks you're at my house. If you tell him, then he'll tell my dad who thinks I'm at your house."

"Well, how about Vincent? Should I call him?"

We ordered our drinks and took a seat close to the pickup counter. The two continued their argument about what to do about the car following them around. They called their friends to drive their car home and drop them off so they could feel safe. Robbie and I exchanged looks, debating on whether we should continue to follow them or let them go home and get some sleep.

Without a word and a shrug of our shoulders, we decided they'd had enough. As we drank our drinks in Robbie's car, their car passed by, driven by a boy who seemed too young to even have a license. Another boy about their age, maybe a little older, followed behind that car. One girl was in the passenger seat. I assumed the other was in the back seat. They looked around at all the cars in the parking lot trying to identify their stalkers. They looked everywhere but their eyes seemed to skip Robbie and me as if we were invisible to them. Their taillights vanished down the road and Robbie and I burst into laughter.

After they left, we headed home, calling it a night. That was more than enough excitement.

A few more nights passed before we found ourselves once again cruising around Milpitas. We drove by the houses of ex-girlfriends. I pointed out suitable spots to smoke weed or take a girl.

We were bored, and nothing seemed interesting in the night's dark. We finished a cheap dinner from a drive thru where he fumbled a shitty pickup line to a mediocre-looking cashier. Then we picked up a pack of smokes, counting out a handful of coins between the two of us to check if we had enough. We did, with a whole ten cents left over. The friends we had were out and about, not haunting their usual spots. I was the only one not old enough to go out drinking and clubbing. They didn't like Robbie. Most people didn't. With the night looking more and more like a bust, we headed home. As he rounded a turn, we came to a stop sign. We looked each way, trying to figure out where to go. Then a car pulled up behind us and honked their horn for us to go. They flashed their high beams. It was a pickup truck, and it seemed like an older man sat behind the wheel.

Robbie and I exchanged a look that promised to make the night more interesting. The truck had their right blinker on, so we turned right and stuck to the inside lane. The truck blasted past us, revving their engine as it shot down the road ahead of us.

Without exchanging a word, Robbie pressed the gas, and the pursuit started. This driver caught on faster than I expected. It was only three turns and a traffic light before they tested us. I don't want to give them too much credit. We were out in the suburbs, so it was easier to notice when a car took all the same turns as you, especially at night with our headlights shining into his window.

They sped up, darted through a light as it turned yellow, then took an immediate turn.

I told Robbie not to. It was too obvious and too aggressive. Let them go before it gets out of hand. He didn't listen. We darted through the light behind them, followed with their immediate right, then they turned left last second as we approached their tail. We missed the turn and circled back, then took the same turn.

We figured they had gotten away. They were smart. Paranoid maybe. Part of me wondered if they may have been hiding something. Maybe they expected a tail and knew how to lose one.

I remembered Richard Ramirez, the Night Stalker. He'd drive around, bored, looking for someone to hurt. At some point in the night, he let his truck roll to a stop in a random neighborhood. Wherever it stopped, he'd rape and kill everyone inside. Could it be a modern-day Richard Ramirez? What if we followed them while they kidnapped a young girl, snatching her from her driveway after her boyfriend dropped her off? What would we do? Suppose that driver had some poor girl tied up, and they thought we were the police?

Either way, the truck had won. We were ready to give up after passing down a few streets and not seeing them.

But we needed the last laugh.

As we made our way down the street again where we lost them, we scanned the cars in the driveways. As we came to a cross street, we slowed and debated on which way they might have gone.

As we rolled by, I glanced out my window and saw the truck. The driver was there, staring at me. We held eye contact for a moment. A look of rage crept across his face. For a moment, I froze. I can't put into words the feeling I had. He didn't frighten me. I didn't feel the same excitement I had when we followed the girls a few nights before. It felt as if the driver of the truck was everything in the world I despised. My parents, teachers, and classmates were all rolled into one person: him. He glared at me like I was in the wrong, but I should have been the one furious. He spoiled our game and made fools of us because he caught on so fast.

As we continued to drive past, the driver started his truck. He peeled out behind us and sped up to our bumper. Robbie pressed the gas. His Civic was too fast, too agile for the truck to keep up. We took sudden turns and swerved and sped through lights, the same as the truck did when we followed it.

Eventually, we lost the truck and pulled over to the side of the road and hid among a line of parked cars. We sat there, defeated. We ran scared. The truck driver won.

We waited a few minutes to see if the truck meandered by looking for us. We sat in silence. Neither one of us wanted to admit that we didn't just lose; we got scared. They could have our license plate number. For all we knew, the police were on their way and ready to scour the area with a helicopter overhead until they hunted us down and locked us up. Or worse, the truck driver could have been a murderer, and he was on the prowl, hunting for us as we terrorized teenage boba girls. As time passed, we realized it was done. The night was over. Time to go home. We left that little neighborhood, wondering about the truck's destination, hoping to never see it again.

After Robbie dropped me off, I laid in bed staring at the ceiling. I recited the license plate of that truck repeatedly, committing it to memory.

Just in case.

We didn't play the game again for about two months. The close call with the truck could have brought trouble we didn't want. Any time there was a knock on the door, we were sure it was the police looking for us.

As the months passed, no cops showed up. Robbie was even volunteering with the police department around that time, training to be a junior police officer or whatever they called it. One weekend, he dedicated his time to working on a sting operation by the Milpitas Police. He posted in front of a liquor store and asked people to buy him alcohol. He drove his car there and yet, with a dozen cops watching him, none of them said a word.

One bored night, months after our run in with the truck driver, we started playing our game again. We took it easy, staying back and acting like actual killers trying not to be spotted. Sometimes we'd disagree on the best way to play. We could let ourselves be seen and watch them run. That was Robbie's favorite way to play. Or we can play it coy and see how far we go before they notice. I liked it that way better, but I had to admit, the game dragged on. Most people don't assume they're being followed, so they pay no attention to the random car a few feet back following their every move. They drive on, living their lives and pay us no mind. It was interesting, however, to get an insight into the lives of strangers.

Some were smarter than others. Some were reckless. One driver blasted through a red light, narrowly avoiding a collision to get away from us. We followed one car throughout the suburbs and watched them do a drug deal, then head across town to a party. Robbie and I went into the party and helped ourselves to a few drinks, then left without a word to anyone. No one even noticed, not even the guy we followed there. Robbie photobombed a group selfie, throwing his arm around our target.

One driver turned into a dead end. He and his friend got out of the car and started throwing up gang signs. We laughed in their faces, stepping out of the car but keeping our faces hidden. We flashed the knives we carried. They put their hands up and backed away. We knew we got lucky. This was Milpitas. They weren't real gangsters and didn't carry guns. A few miles further south, and it would have been a different story.

I carried a knife for as long as I could remember. My stepfather handed it to me a while back and told me to hold on to it just in case I ever needed it. He left shortly after, but the knife stayed with me. Holding it made me feel powerful. It was a dull little knife, but it opened my eyes to a new hobby. My knife collection had grown into the dozens. I had hidden knives, novelty blades that wouldn't hurt a fly, and I had some real ugly bastards that could gut a bear if needed. I lent a few knives to Robbie that I eventually let him keep as my collection grew too large to hide from my mom.

Days came and went. Occasionally, we'd find a fun one to follow, like the two girls from the boba shop. We even drove by that boba shop a few times to see if we could find them and follow them home. Robbie joked about following them home and raping them. I couldn't tell if he was serious. I spotted their car once at the shop, but I didn't tell him.

Then one night, bored once again, we thought back to that truck that got away. I still remembered the license plate number.

"I don't know why," I said. "But none of these are as fun as those two girls, or that old man. There was something about the man in the truck. I don't know what it was."

"Do you want to see if we can find him again?" Robbie asked.

"Find him? Where? He never went home."

"No, but he was driving around the suburbs late at night. Chances are he was almost home or leaving home."

"So, what, we drive around that area and look for his truck parked in the driveway?"

"Or maybe he'll be driving around and we can follow him again."

"What if he's parked in his garage or something?"

"What if he isn't?"

The question hung in the air as I considered it. We were driving around with nothing else to do. The few cars we followed that night were nothing special. None of them noticed their tails, and the others jumped onto the freeway where we didn't like to follow. Too many cars moving too fast. It wasn't as fun.

"Alright," I said. "Let's do it. You remember the neighborhood?"

"Yeah, I went on a ride along in that neighborhood the other day."

"You're still doing that?"

"Sometimes, but nothing ever really happens."

They headed back to the neighborhood, where they first spotted the truck. As they drove around, I recognized it from that night. We passed the spot where that truck pulled over. We thought it might be where the driver lived and maybe he realized we were still following him and he didn't want us to know that's where he lived. There was no truck on that street except one owned by a landscaping company.

We backtracked to where we first saw the truck a few streets and an intersection away. I recognized that neighborhood too. Not from that night, but because I dated a girl who lived near there. That's when I realized why I hated the man so much.

"Shit," I said aloud.

"What?" Robbie asked. "You see the truck?"

"No, but I know where we can find it. Turn left up there."

"What do you mean?"

"I know who he is now. It's why I was so angry when I saw him. I've seen him before."

"Do you think he'd recognize you?"

"No way. Never met him. Saw him a few times from a distance. I dated this girl in high school that lived a street over from him. Whenever she walked home or to school, he'd be outside and say gross, creepy shit to her whenever she walked by."

"Like what?"

"Just telling her shit like she looks pretty, or he liked her shirt, or he liked her shorts. I know, it doesn't sound too bad, but it's different when a fifty-year-old guy says it to a sixteen-year-old teenager. Imagine him looking at someone's chest and she has some cleavage showing, and he's telling her likes her shirt."

"Oh, yeah. That's creepy."

"Turn right over there."

Robbie turned right, then right there on the corner, they saw the truck. I read the license plate to confirm it.

"That's it," I said.

"Shit. It is," Robbie said.

"Where does your ex live from here?"

"Just down that street over there. Bus stop is that way. That's why she always had to walk by."

"You sure he wouldn't recognize you?"

"Never seen him up close. He's never seen me at all. I always went a different way when I came over because I lived on Terra Bella."

Robbie drove past the house and pulled over down the road, parking between a row of cars next to a high fence. I pointed it out as another good place to park to smoke or have sex if he ever gets a girl. Robbie rolled his eyes because he knew he had no use for that information. Part of me knew I talked about that stuff just to rub it into his face. It was the same way he'd show me all the expensive things he'd buy. He once invited me over to "see something" which turned out to be a new gaming console that was just released and sold out. He bought it for twice as much online and made sure I knew it. Then he played a game for two hours without letting me play. It was a toxic friendship, but it was one that worked for the time being when no one else wanted to hang out with us.

For about forty minutes, we sat in the car watching the house with nothing really in mind. We talked about how I met my ex who lived nearby and why and when we broke up. We talked about movies and music and the conversation wandered as aimlessly as our late night drives.

Then, as we watched the house in the rearview, the front door opened and the old man waddled out and climbed into his truck.

Robbie and I went silent. We knew we had no choice. We had to follow him.

The truck started up and the old man pulled out of the driveway and drove past us. We ducked in our seats, but he passed by without a second thought. Robbie started the car and pulled out of the hiding spot. We kept our distance at first. Last time, this guy was alert. He caught on pretty fast and there was no doubt he'd catch on.

The truck stopped at a light. He stared at us through his rearview. I pretended to be pointing something out and Robbie pretended to be interested. We wanted to be obvious, yet inconspicuous. We wanted him to wonder if he was being followed but not know for sure. He kept his eyes on us and drove slowly. Every time he caught on to us, we let him get further ahead. Sometimes we turned down streets we recognized if we knew we could make our way back to the same road as him later on. We went around that neighborhood until finally he stopped at another house. We pulled over down the street and watched.

He got out of his truck and knocked on the door. There was no answer. He wandered around the property, looking over his shoulder as he did. He vanished into the darkness at the side of the house.

"Is he breaking into this house?" Robbie asked.

"I don't know. It looks like it. What did we get ourselves into?" I asked.

"What if he did?"

"What if he's a killer?"

"Why would you say that? That's even worse!"

"You never know with people like that."

"People like what?"

"Old white men. It's always old white men. Unless it's not, but it usually is."

"You mean you think he's a serial killer?"

"Possibly."

"Then why are we following him?"

"Dude, who knows? He's probably watering someone's plants while they're away."

"Then why'd he knock? Why is he watering their plants at 11pm?"

"Wait, look!" I said.

The front door opened. Darkness inside the door. The old man stepped out and into the porch light. It cast dark shadows across his face. He closed the door behind him, not bothering to double check if it was locked.

"Maybe someone is inside," I said.

"Maybe someone is dead inside," Robbie said.

The old man made his way back to his truck, turned it on and took off down the street.

"Are we still doing this?" Robbie asked as if he didn't know the answer.

"We don't have to if you don't want to," I said.

Robbie didn't reply. He started the car and took off after the truck. We caught up to him down the road.

It took about three miles before he showed any sort of suspicion. He took a sharp turn, ran through a stop sign with cars waiting at the other sides, then blasted through a red light. It didn't matter though; we knew where he lived. Whenever he lost us, we followed the roads toward his house and caught up to him. Then he'd try it again, and we'd find him again. Finally, a few blocks from his house, he did the same thing he did the first time he lost us.

He took a sharp turn down a street that loops around and back to the main road. We knew he'd park on the side of the road waiting for us to drift by, so instead, we headed to where he headed. His home.

We waited outside his house for fifteen minutes until he pulled into his driveway. He didn't seem to notice our car parked across the street in the row of his neighbors' cars. The car was empty anyway.

The streetlight by his house was out, so it was especially dark in that area. The driveway to his house was dark and lined with bushes and unkempt trees.

He pulled into the driveway and stepped out of his truck with a groan. He locked it behind him and waddled to his front door in the dark. Something was wrong with his leg, and he dragged his right foot behind him as he walked. He fumbled with his keys in the dark until he found the right one. As he slid the key into the doorknob, he heard something shuffle behind him in the driveway. He turned around, but he couldn't see me. He was old. His eyes didn't work as well at night. And he was slow. That's why we hated him. We despised him for being weak. He was weak, and he outsmarted us. He escaped us and made fools of us, so we had to make a fool of him.

We drew our knives and stepped close behind him.

I stabbed him first. I got him somewhere in the back. He tried to scream, but I put a gloved hand over his mouth as Robbie stabbed him next. The man's fingers wrapped around mine as he tried to pry my hand away from his mouth. I was too strong.

We stabbed him again and again until he fell to the ground, then we stabbed more and more. I knew he died halfway through the attack, but we needed to be sure. He'd seen our car. He might identify us. I stabbed him in the throat. Blood seeped out of his neck and soaked the front of his shirt.

We slinked back to our car under cover of darkness. Robbie started the engine and pulled out and drove me home. I showered, washed my clothes, soaked them in bleach and threw them into the dumpster. He did the same and told me we were lucky not to get any blood in his car. His dad would have been mad.

We kept a low profile, once again expecting that inevitable knock at the door with an army of cops on the other side. That knock never came.

Six months later, Robbie and I were once again cruising around Milpitas when a car full of young girls cut us off on Calaveras, heading into the suburbs. I smiled at Robbie.

He smiled back and merged into that car's lane.

| 15 |

TEETH

I know they aren't hers, but I'm too scared to ask where she keeps getting them. I take the teeth from under her pillow and leave a crisp $1.

| 16 |

MARY'S TAVERN

The moon climbed the felt canvas of the sky, mingling with the starry specks of glitter in the distance. Whiffs of flour floated in the air, dancing away from the shoulders of laborers emerging from the nearby flour mill. An early night in a cold, shadowy winter. Weary and parched, the laborers streamed out in lines, finding solace at Mary's Tavern on the outskirts of town. They were eager to forget their days and warm their blood with booze and food. Hidden among the weary workers was a stranger to the small town.

The stolen garments hung off Lee's wiry body. He cinched up a rope he used as a belt to keep his pants from falling. His hands explored the pockets, revealing a wallet bearing an ID that bore no resemblance to him and a credit card that he assumed had already been canceled by the rightful owner.

Lee took a stool at the end of the bar and opened a tab, passing the stolen credit card to Mary herself. Amidst the patrons, who sported robust frames and protruding bellies, Lee stood noticeably shorter, an outlier in the establishment. His facial hair was a patchy mess. A grimy black mop of hair sat atop his head, brushed into place with his dirty fingers. His eyes darted around the bar, studying everyone's face.

Most didn't notice the odd man. Others glanced back at him, then moved on. A few snickered at the strange outsider. The opinions of these people mattered little to him. They probably considered him homeless or a transient. Hoping to evade attention, he yearned for a swift dismissal, a wish to avoid trouble — at least for the time being.

The lights cast an unflattering amber glow, unmasking wrinkles, gray hairs, drooping eyelids and tired creases. Their reflections were unwelcome reminders of time lost and lives wasted. To avoid that exhausted reflection staring up at them in the bottom of their cups, they made sure to never let their glasses run empty.

The aroma of flour mingled with sweat before the scent surrendered to that of fried fare and spilled brew. Orders flew out of the bustling kitchen. Beer filled cups; kegs ran dry. People laughed. Some cried.

As the night wore on, some drank slower. Others drank more. They had nowhere to go or nowhere they wanted to be. Crumbling walls. Empty refrigerators. Hungry children. Another drink to make it all go away.

Lee drank his beer and finished a burger with a side of fries. He lost track of how long he was there, but knew he couldn't stay for much longer. His ruse would soon end. He shifted his gaze to the alien squeaky toy hanging over the cash register. It had green skin, an almond-shaped head and bulging black eyes. As his eyes wandered around the bar, he noticed more alien memorabilia scattered throughout. He let out a chuckle.

The stool next to Lee cleared out. Two seats over was an older man with the name Billy scrawled across his mechanic's coveralls. The fingers wrapped around his near-empty beer bore witness to a lifetime of hard labor, each mark a testament to his toil. His white ponytail stood high on his head and a yellow stain marked his short beard. Beside his beer, an alien-headed keychain dangled from a set of keys.

"What's so funny?" Billy asked. "Not a fan of this place or something?"

"What's with all the alien stuff around here?" Lee asked.

"Where you from?" Billy asked.

"What do you mean?"

"Where are you from, you know, originally?"

"Providence."

"Oh yeah? Where's that?"

"Rhode Island."

"Island? In the Pacific?"

"It's a state," Lee said, rolling his eyes. "Below Massachusetts."

"No, I mean originally," Billy said, rolling his eyes in return.

"I was born there."

"Your parents? Where are they from?"

"Rhode Island too. Glocester though — not Providence."

"Look, I mean no offense. We just don't get very many of you people around here."

"I can tell. My name is Lee."

He extended a hand for a shake. Billy screeched his stool back and moved to the one beside Lee, taking his hand and giving it a thorough shake.

"Lee, huh?"

"Named after Bruce Lee," Lee said. "They wanted a Chinese name for me, but neither of them knew any Chinese."

"That's exceptional," Billy said. "I love Bruce Lee. Green Hornet, you know? I loved that show. Say, Lee, you want to make some friends in town? You can start by buying them a beer. Goes a long way."

"You want me to buy you a beer?" Lee asked.

"Only if you don't have any cigarettes to offer," Billy said, as if he was doing Lee the favor.

Music lulled over the broken speakers, audible only to those who strained their ears to listen. Lee, his head afloat in a haze from the beer, couldn't recognize the song, but he tried his best to hum along. Mary came by and collected Lee's bottles. She cast an assessing glance at him, then exchanged a look with Billy that seemed to convey, "Check out this guy."

"Mary," Billy said, directing her attention to the cigarettes behind the bar. Mary shot him a look of disapproval, but retrieved the pack and held it out for him as she shook her head.

"You sure about this?" Mary asked.

"You think you could sell me one or two loosies?" Billy asked. He counted out the few bills in his wallet.

"You know I can't do that, Billy."

"I know, I know. Well, I shouldn't."

"Can I have another beer?" Lee interrupted. "Two actually. One for Billy. And another burger for me, but with onion rings this time."

"Kitchen is about to close," Mary said.

"In that case, can I order two?" Lee asked. "Fries with one, onion rings with the other."

Billy's eyebrows perked up. A bell rang from the kitchen. Mary hesitated, deliberating, her gaze drawn to the pickup window where a tray of fries awaited. With a heavy sigh, she scribbled his order down.

"I'll see if the cook can make it in time before they close up," Mary said as she walked away. Billy watched her walk away and raised his eyebrows to Lee. Lee wasn't sure why Billy thought he'd share an interest in Mary. Mary was short, with legs like tree trunks and a belly the size of a keg. She had a permanent scowl smeared across her face with thick makeup painted on.

Mary returned from the kitchen and grabbed Lee a bottle of beer, one for Billy too. Popping them open, she placed them on the bar, the audible fizz of the opening revealing a slight mishap in her haste.

"Orders in," Mary said. "Nothing else after that. Kitchen is closed."

"Thanks," Lee said.

Mary cleared empty tables, returning to the bar with an armful of used beer mugs and shot glasses that clinked as she emptied them into the wash station. Lee downed his beer, slamming the empty bottle onto the counter and letting out a belch. Mary observed this with an expression of distaste. He nodded for another, to which she sighed again and fetched another beer.

"I don't want to be cleaning nothing up if I can avoid it. Understand? Take it easy," Mary said.

Billy chuckled at the eager newcomer. Lee nodded and tipped his bottle toward her. He took a small sip of his new beer. Lee assumed Billy's mission was complete with the free beer and he'd move away. Instead, he sat beside Lee in a contemplative quiet. Every so often he'd open his mouth to say something, then shake his head and take another sip. Lee kept to himself, staring into the eyes of the alien squeaky toy by the register. The stolen credit card he gave Mary when he opened his tab sat a short distance below it.

A bell chimed. Lee drooled at the sight of his burgers, their aroma wafting over as Mary delivered them. He devoured the burgers, fries and onion rings before finishing the rest of his beer and ordering another. Mary obliged, then made her way to the cash register and punched in his order.

"You ready to close out?" she asked. She only asked Lee. Everyone else in the bar seemed welcome to take their time finishing their drinks and paying their tabs.

"Sure, but the credit card I gave you might not work. It's stolen," Lee said.

If Mary had a smile before he said that, it would have faded at that moment. She ran the card only to be met with a declined transaction.

"How do you plan to pay?" Mary asked, hand on hip.

"I don't," Lee said.

Lee stared back at Mary, unflinching against her death stare.

"You came in here and ordered all this, and you don't have any money?" Mary's voice attracted the attention of nearby patrons. Their conversations dropped to a noticeable whisper.

"Exactly," Lee said. "No money and no intention of paying."

"John," Mary called out.

Another patron, who until then sat on a stool by the door, put his beer down and joined the conversation.

"What's the problem here?" John asked.

Billy inched away from Lee in his seat, the look on his face showing his regret at making a new friend.

"Son," Mary said to Lee. "How did you expect to cover this with no money?"

"I didn't think that far ahead," Lee said.

He smiled at Mary and John. He glanced at Billy, but Billy kept his eyes on the beer in his hand. Neither of them smiled back. Mary turned to Billy and made sure he felt her eyes drilling into him until he finally met her stare.

"Hey, I don't know this guy," Billy said. "He offered to buy me a beer. Why would I say no?"

"You're paying for that beer yourself, Billy," Mary said.

Billy's face turned pale, and he nodded, his gaze fixed on the cigarettes behind the bar.

"Where are you from?" John asked. "Ain't seen you 'round here before."

"Providence," Billy said, answering before Lee had the chance. "Rhode Island."

"So, you guys are good friends, then?" John asked.

"No, I don't —"

"Then mind your business," John said.

Billy remained silent, offering a nod that conveyed a blend of compliance and agreement.

"Well, we're going to have to figure something out, aren't we?" Mary asked. "How do you want to work this off?"

"What's his bill?" John asked.

"$92.76," Mary said. "Not sure how things work in Providence, but this kind of money can't go ignored. You're going to have to figure out a way to pay this," Mary said.

"Is that calendar right?" Lee asked. He pointed to a calendar in the bar's corner. It had a picture of a woman in a camouflage bikini leaning over an engine. Mary nodded.

"Yeah," she said. "That's the right date."

"See, I've been gone for a while," Lee said. "Aliens abducted me."

Billy couldn't help but let a laugh slip out. The last of the uninvested patrons ended their conversations, and all eyes were on the commotion at the bar.

"It's true," Lee said to everyone. "I was abducted. I just got back."

Mary didn't laugh. Billy noticed her scowl and stopped laughing.

"This isn't funny," Mary said.

"I'm not joking," Lee said.

"You need to pay this bill. Now."

"I really don't have any money."

"John?"

John's response was swift; he grabbed Lee's arm and yanked him off his stool, causing it to tip and clatter to the floor. The sudden action reverberated through the bar. The room's only sounds were the faint humming of neon signs and the fractured melodies emanating from the broken speakers.

John grabbed Lee by the shoulder and spun him around, then shoved him against the bar with force. Lee grunted as the bar's edge rammed into his stomach and forced out all his air. He knocked one of his empty bottles to the floor. The glass shattered, even louder in the now-silent establishment.

John ran his hands over Lee, patting him down for a stray wallet in the baggy clothes. He found one, checked the ID inside it and shook his head. Mary snatched it from his hand, reviewed it and shook her head in unison.

"Didn't you check this when he walked in?"

"Must've missed him."

"What do I pay you for?"

"You don't."

"Well, then. I see why."

He felt something and reached into Lee's pocket and pulled out a small metal device with buttons. John scrutinized the object before passing it to Mary, who examined it briefly before shrugging.

"What is this?" Mary asked.

"It's from the aliens," Lee said.

A murmur of amusement rippled through the crowd, accompanied by a few chuckles.

"I'm calling Harris," Mary said. She walked away and into the back office, leaving the device on the bar.

"Harris?" Lee asked, turning to Billy with raised eyebrows.

"Officer Harris. She's calling the police," Billy said.

"Oh, that's fine."

"You're going to stay here and wait for him," John said, jabbing Lee in the chest with his finger, harder than necessary.

Lee retrieved the device and slipped it back into his pocket, patting the outside of his pants to assure himself it was safe.

"I'm not going anywhere," Lee said. "Not yet."

"You have a name?" John asked, arms folded.

He puffed his chest and flexed his arms. John seemed to think he was tougher than he looked.

"Lee," he answered.

"Well, Lee, you seem to think we're playing around. If this is some sort of joke, I think we've heard enough. Just pay your tab and be on your way and don't come back here. Got it?"

"I'm not joking," Lee said, trying not to laugh. "Aliens took me. I don't have any money."

"Aliens, huh?" John asked, rolling his eyes.

"Aliens," Lee said. He looked around at the bar. Eyes followed his every movement. "Everyone loves a good bar story."

Billy mumbled to himself. Lee didn't quite catch what he said, but he understood the doubt in Billy's voice.

"What's with all the alien decor?" Lee asked, nodding to the alien-themed squeaky toys.

A moment of unease passed between John and Billy. Just as Mary emerged from the back office, she caught wind of the conversation, her eyes darting away from Lee's gaze.

"Just a fun thing around these parts." Billy scratched the yellow stain on his beard as his eyes wandered over from the cigarettes to the squeaky toy. "From a long time ago. People thought they saw something. Mary's dad —"

"Just a gimmick nowadays," Mary said. "Nothing more."

Lee nodded, then looked around at the nosy patrons, waiting for a better explanation of why he had no money to pay his tab.

"They took me about three months ago," Lee said to anyone who might be listening.

"That right?" John asked. Lee turned to John.

"It's a hard thing to believe," Lee said, nodding at his own words. "I didn't much believe it myself when it first happened."

Lee settled back onto his stool, taking a sip from his beer, only to find it empty. Pushing it toward Mary, he raised his eyebrows in a silent request for another.

Exasperated, Mary rolled her eyes and discarded the empty bottle into a trash can.

"Tell you what," Lee said, looking between Billy, John and Mary. "If I convince you all that aliens abducted me, I don't have to pay my tab."

"No deal," Mary said. "Harris is on his way. You stay put until he gets here."

Mary tended to the glassware, organizing receipts, and wiping surfaces. Despite her tasks, she kept her head tilted toward the ongoing conversation. Lee raised his voice, ensuring Mary could hear him.

"Fine, we can let Officer Harris decide how to handle my bill when he gets here. Until then, I want to tell you what happened. How about that? If, by some miracle, you believe me and don't want to have Officer Harris take me away, we'll call it even."

"You ain't convincing me of anything," Mary said. "John, don't let him leave without Officer Harris."

"Better tell your story," Billy said.

Seating himself next to Lee, John downed the rest of his beer.

"A while back, my brother died," Lee said. "A drunk driver in a pickup plowed right through him. Driver got away with it. Cops didn't even care. It was rough for my family. He was the golden child."

Lee's voice trailed off as he gazed at the device in his hand, unaware that he had taken it out of his pocket and was fiddling with it. He shoved it back into his pocket and cleared his throat.

"He was my best friend, and I was definitely not the golden child. I was the screw up. I tried to figure out my life, but nothing seemed to work for me. It hurt. He always had my back. So, after his funeral, I took off. I drove and drove, destination unknown, unsure of where I was headed or what I was doing. And then it happened. I was on an empty road, surrounded by darkness in the dead of night. A white light flooded my car, illuminating everything around me

"There was a resonating, deep hum. I floated out of my seat. I could see and hear and feel everything, but I couldn't move. My body felt like pins and needles. Like when your leg falls asleep and gets all tingly? That's how I felt. It was weird. I sort of vibrated through my seatbelt and through the roof of my car."

"That's crazy," Billy said.

He chuckled to himself, still eyeing the pack of smokes behind the bar. Mary followed his eyes and saw what he was staring at. She took the pack and hid it behind the register. Billy nodded, and she shot back an unapproving smirk.

"I was so scared and overwhelmed that I think I had an anxiety attack and passed out," Lee said. "I woke up in this room, a giant auditorium filled with people. Some of them were awake. Some were waking up at the same time as me. There were about a hundred of us. Wall to wall, filled with people. No one knew what was happening. Then these things, these robots, hovered over the crowd. It was a ball with an antenna sticking out of it. Kind of looked like the torture droids from *Star Wars* but was shiny and black with a blue light on the front. On the bottom, it had one of those claw things, like in those machines where you win stuffed animals.

"It buzzed around with this weird humming noise and this laser scanned people in the room. It scanned everyone. So, when it scanned me, it buzzed. Not the same buzzing noise it was making before. This was more like the buzzer when someone guesses wrong on a game show.

"The claw on the bottom shot out and grabbed my torso. It squeezed me tight and yanked me off the ground. I didn't realize how big it was until this happened. It pulled me up and flew me out of the room. I see all these people reaching out to grab me and help me, but I'm too high up and the thing is moving too fast. And then, as I thought I was going to die —"

The door to the bar opened. An officer walked in. An audible groan echoed through the room, and Mary pointed Lee out to the officer.

"There he is," Mary said to the officer.

"I hear you don't want to pay your tab," Officer Harris said to Lee.

Harris placed his hand on the holster of his gun. Harris was large. More fat than muscle, but still intimidating . Bald-headed and clean-shaven, Harris stood head and shoulders above Lee, exuding an aura of self-importance.

"I want to pay my tab," Lee said. "I just don't have any money."

"C'mon, Mary. At least let him finish the story," Billy interjected.

"Nope," Mary said. "He's trying to con you guys into paying his tab, that's all."

"Mary says you gotta go, you gotta go," Officer Harris said.

"Alright, alright," Lee said. He stood with his hands in the air to keep the peace.

Someone in the tavern booed the officer, but Lee couldn't see who.

"Seems like maybe a few folks around here might pay his tab if they hear him out. Would save me the paperwork if they do."

Billy booed. A few more patrons in earshot joined in. Lee hadn't realized how large his audience had grown.

"Get him out," Mary shouted over the drunken booing. Harris pulled Lee by the arm, toward the door as the booing followed.

"Hey, hey!" Harris yelled. The crowd stopped. "Mary's gotta make herself a living and she can't do it by giving out free food and beer."

"And I don't want y'all paying for this man's food, you hear me? That isn't the point." Mary said, "You pick up his tab, then what? People show up with stories about aliens and expect a free meal?"

"Aliens?" Harris said. His face turned pale.

"That's why I have no money, Officer," Lee said. "Aliens abducted me."

"He was right in the middle of the story, Harris," Billy said.

"Officer Harris, Billy."

"Officer Harris, sorry."

"Do you believe in aliens, Officer Harris?" Lee asked.

"Don't get me started," Harris said. "C'mon, Billy. Don't feed into this guy's crap."

"Harris, are you going to take him or what?" Mary asked.

Harris' grip loosened as he looked around at the patrons. A few had risen from their seats and moved closer to Harris to get a better view of the action. Harris scanned their anxious faces then glanced up at the alien squeaky toy over the register. His eyes went blank as he stared at it, deep in thought.

"Okay, how about this?" Lee said, easing out of Harris' distracted grip and sidestepping away. "I want to tell my story. When I'm done, you can take me away."

"Look, I'm not —"

"You telling me you never saw something weird around here, officer? Abandoned cars. Missing persons. Bright lights in the night. If anyone ever saw anything, it would have been you."

Harris muttered beneath his breath. His hands trembled as they fumbled around his body, looking for a comfortable position.

"Oh, Hell," Harris said, his voice strained as he leaned on the counter, rubbing his eyes with weariness. "It would save me a mountain of paperwork if I don't take him. Maybe some of these eager beavers would like to pitch in to pay his tab by the time he's done telling his story."

"Screw it," Mary said. "Whatever. I mean, I run this place, but this guy has a story about aliens, so I guess that's the end of discussion. When he's done, I want him gone. I want that paperwork filed. I want my money and I'm taking down all these stupid alien toys my dad hung up."

She threw her hands in the air in surrender and rolled her eyes as she slammed cups into the bar sink.

"Thank you," Lee said.

"Two more beers," a patron said. He slapped a ten-dollar bill onto the bar. Mary obliged. The patron handed one to Lee and kept the other for himself. Mary rolled her eyes, but money was money. Though, if she knew he was going to buy Lee a beer, she would have kept the money and put it toward a beer he already drank.

The patron shifted a seat nearby to better watch Lee tell the story. He had been listening, but now he was fully engaged.

Of the twenty left in the bar, about a dozen pulled up seats near Lee. A few more ordered drinks. With the audience captivated, Mary resumed her role as bartender, and a few patrons even left extra tips — after all, a well-told tale could be a boon for business.

"You want coffee?" she asked Harris, letting her anger melt.

"Please," Harris said.

"Alright, go on," Billy said, scratching his beard.

"Where was I?" Lee asked himself. He did a quick summary for Officer Harris before jumping back to where he left off. "Right, this robot had me ensnared in its grip, hurtling through a tunnel. It dropped me off in another room. It was a lot smaller. There were a couple of people there, then more got dropped off right after me. We were all confused. This door opened, and these little alien guys came in. They could have been women; I honestly don't know. It was all smooth down there. None of them wore clothing. The people spoke broken English. They were exactly how those old timey movies made them. Short, gray/green with big black eyes. They still looked kind of humanoid, with ten fingers and toes.

"They separated us, pointing at me, then at a spot on the floor, then at me, then back to the floor. There were maybe eight of us and we each had a few of the little guys telling us to stand in certain spots. So, I mean, what choice did we have? We stood in those spots. This glass chamber came up out of the floor and trapped us. Some of us started freaking out and screaming and pounding on the glass. One guy was so calm, it was scary. He stared into the distance as everyone else panicked. I was so terrified I pissed my pants. My hands were shaking. They were cold. So cold. I was sweating even though it wasn't hot. Then the alien started tapping on the glass. At least, that's what I thought he was doing, but then this screen popped up on the glass of the chamber. It was an x-ray of my body. There was this black fuzzy thing over my chest.

"I understood then. Cancer. Lung cancer. I had been feeling off, plagued by a persistent cough that wouldn't abate. I had chest pains for a few months. Never had insurance, never had it looked at. From the image, the guy — sorry, the alien — showed me it looked pretty bad."

The bar grew silent with Lee's revelation. Even he felt his voice drop as he spoke. The excitement of the robots and the abduction went away. He thought back to that moment of dread when the alien gave him his diagnosis. Whatever the aliens had in store for him became trivial.

"I stopped shaking. My fear went away. Like, I was about to die, and it was going to be okay. I don't know why. Maybe they were pumping anesthesia into that tube. He pointed to me, then to himself and circled his chest with his finger, then pointed back to the image on the glass. I nodded my head, you know, telling him I understood. He pressed a few buttons, then walked away. I thought that was it. The aliens left. That's when I figured it out. Whatever the aliens wanted us for, I wasn't worthy. I was sick. I figured they'd kill us or return us or something.

"I was wrong. Dead wrong. The tubes lit up with this bright green light. It sounded like a vacuum cleaner was going off, but louder. My body shook. I started coughing uncontrollably. I couldn't breathe. The tube was too small. I couldn't fall to the floor. Instead, I collapsed against the tube as the light pulsed. It felt like I was a fish and there was a fishhook in my chest and the fisherman was trying to yank it out. Then it halted. My ears rang, my throat was sore. We all looked around. A woman bled from her, you know, her pants area. Then I felt this heavy feeling on my chest, and I started vomiting blood. It sprayed out onto the tube."

Lee looked around at the engaged crowd. Seeing someone cough up a rotten tumor didn't make polite conversation. He spared the grosser details and skipped ahead in his story as he finished the beer the patron gave him.

"The tubes filled with water. I thought I was going to drown. It drained right after, though. Cleaned us all off. Then it zapped us. Everything got really warm, a kind of fuzzy feeling, for a second and we were all dry. The aliens came back and scanned us again. He seemed so happy when he showed me. The cancer? Gone. My lungs? All clear. They cured me.

The sadness that filled the bar a moment ago lifted and the patrons scooted closer, wide-eyed and eager, intrigued by Lee's story.

"The tubes lifted, and the aliens guided us down this hallway and back into that big room with people, but it was empty. There was a door on the other side of the room.

They led us there. I asked the alien where we were going, to which he responded something like 'all better now, time for harvest.' I repeated, 'harvest?' Then, I heard the screams.

"We turned the corner, and this door was open and there was this woman on a gurney, and they mounted this machine on the ceiling, and it cut her open, ripping her organs out. Blood spilled onto the floor. She saw me looking at her as the aliens walked us through the corridor or tunnel or whatever it's called. I don't know how she was still alive, but she screamed and screamed until she couldn't scream anymore."

A hush fell over the bar, and Mary, staring at Lee, was so captivated she forgot about her receipts. He pushed his empty bottle toward Mary. She took it and tossed it in the trash. She didn't offer another one.

"In that moment, panic gripped us. The pieces fell into place. They healed our cancers to harvest our organs. We weren't special; they weren't benevolent. They were treating us like commodities, like a farm. Desperation took over. I grabbed one of them and pleaded, 'Please, please, please. Don't do this. You saved us. Let us go, please.' But the aliens shoved us away.

"They were a small business, and they sold human organs for profit. Rich aliens back on their planet bought our organs and ate them as a delicacy. A healthy set of lungs was good money. Couldn't afford to let us go."

"Jesus Christ," Billy said. "That's messed up right there."

"So when they brought me to the operating room, I did the only thing I could think of. I fought."

Everyone inched forward in their seats. They were ready for the grand finale.

"I punched one of them in the face, shoved another one aside and ran away. I didn't know where to go. One of them pulled something from its pocket and fiddled with buttons. I tackled it to the ground, and we grappled for the device. I wrestled it away and took off down an empty hallway as the alarms blared. For all I knew, I was light years away in outer space. I turned a corner, then burst into a room. Big mistake. There were about a dozen sleeping aliens. They jumped up from their beds and pointed weapons at me. Weird weapons. Not shiny and metal like you might expect. I held up this weird metal thing I took from the other guy. But then? Everything went silent. Not just quiet. Deathly silent. I couldn't hear my footsteps. I couldn't hear myself swallow. It was a deep silence, like they vacuumed all noise out. The aliens stayed still. One of them held up a hand and motioned for the aliens to lower their weapons. I tried to move, but the air was thick, like I was wading through quicksand.

"Suddenly, I was back on Earth in the middle of a bright light. Then the light vanished, the ship took off. I was standing there, naked in the middle of nowhere with nothing but this shiny thing I snatched. Three months had gone by. I don't know at which point I lost all that time"

Lee held up the device and showed it off to the awestruck audience.

Surveying the baffled expressions in Mary's Tavern, Lee noticed Mary herself had paused her wiping to gaze at him. Providing no clarification, he added, "That's all."

"I've seen that before," Officer Harris said, face paler than Lee thought possible. "Guy we pulled over. He had one. This was early in my career. Something happened that night. Something bad."

The crowd responded with uneasy chuckles. Lee stood from his stool, shifting his focus to Mary.

"I tried it out once. A coyote was chasing me. I didn't know what it did when I started pressing the buttons, but I think I have it figured out now. That's why I'm here. That's why I don't care about paying. I wanted to find some specific people. People like the bartender who over-serves drinks."

Mary's eyes narrowed. She mumbled to herself, repeating Lee's words, grappling to comprehend their implications. Lee turned to John.

"Or the self-proclaimed security guard who lets drunks stumble off to their cars instead of calling them a ride."

John, too, mumbled the words and struggled to understand what Lee meant by them. Lee turned to Billy.

"I wanted to find the driver who didn't mind getting behind the wheel the night my brother died. The driver who didn't stop to see if he was alright because he was too drunk to see straight. The driver who still hasn't learned his lesson because the police officer on duty let him get away with a slap on the wrist."

Billy's smile melted; his hand trembled. He eyed the empty spot behind the bar where the cigarettes were before Mary moved them. He wanted to run, but his head swam, and he could barely think straight as Lee turned to Officer Harris. Harris placed his hand on his gun.

"I wanted to find the cop who let a drunk driver continue to drive drunk. The cop who excused my brother's death as 'wrong place, wrong time.' Or should I say it how you said it in your police report? You know, the one you filed when you saw a Chinese guy dead on the side of the road? How'd you write it? *'Wong* place, *Wong* time,' right?"

"Alright," Harris said, pulling his cuffs. "I've had enough of this."

Lee pressed the big blue button on the device and aimed it at Harris. Harris drew his weapon, but he wasn't fast enough. In an instant, Harris exploded into a mess of blood and bone. His gun clattered to the ground. Blood sprayed across every onlooker in the bar as they struggled to understand what happened. Lee pointed the device at John and tapped the blue button once more. John exploded, painting the bar with pieces of him. Then Lee looked at Mary. She tried to run, but she slipped on a piece of John's intestines. She rolled across the floor as Lee pressed the button again and she exploded. Patrons ran, some getting in the crossfire of Lee's weapon and exploding as they did, leaving blood and loose flour floating on the air.

At last, the remaining patrons either bolted out the door or succumbed to Lee's device, leaving two people behind; Billy and Lee. Billy nodded at Lee. He eyed the space behind the bar where the cigarettes were, wondering why he even thought he had enough years left in him to make it worth quitting. Then, at the press of a button, he exploded into dust.

The crisp air of a clear autumn night embraced Lee as he emerged from the dingy bar. He took a deep breath, thankful to be able to breathe. He used a cocktail napkin emblazoned with "Mary's Tavern" to dab the blood from his face. Lee looked up at the night sky. He smiled at the stars looking down on him, twinkling away like specks of glitter on a felt canvas.

| 17 |

TRUNK

The wind blows through my hair as the sun sets over the horizon. I slam the brakes and the screaming in the trunk comes to an abrupt stop.

| 18 |

LITTLE LAMB

Weathered and faded graffiti adorned the boarded windows of the decrepit electronics store from days long past. Even the delinquents didn't give this place a second look anymore.

David parked his car in the faded lines of the last remaining parking stall. He flashed his high beams in the direction of the store, as instructed, then he waited. The ticking of his watch blended with the pitter-patter of the growing rain against the roof of his car.

A bright beam of light emerged from the parking lot entrance, swooped around, and stopped facing David's car. He shielded his eyes and squinted to see the seller. A blinding light made his heart sink, fearing it could be a cop. His worries settled as two men crossed in front of the headlights, dragging a small bundle.

David pulled the lever and opened his trunk. His car bobbed as the men loaded his purchase and slammed the trunk shut. David winced at the force of the slam. He always scolded his kids for doing the same. He opened his window and held up his phone, showing the completed transaction details. The man, still in silhouette from the car's bright beams, checked his phone until he nodded in satisfaction.

"Anything I should know?" David called out.

"Don't talk much. But, you know…"

"Maybe that's better, right?"

The man ignored David, climbed back into his van with his accomplice and vanished into the night.

David drove home in silence. He checked his rear-view mirror every few minutes to make sure the trunk didn't pop open. After a few miles, his curiosity got the best of him. He had to make sure he didn't get ripped off by the seller. For all he knew, they plopped a bag of dog food in his trunk.

He pulled over when there were no cars around and, despite the rain, made his way to the trunk. He hit the button on his key fob, which gave way with a light click. There, in the trunk of his car, was a little girl, no older than eight. She was bound and gagged. Unconscious. Delicate in her sleep. With his mind at ease, he whistled a tune the rest of his drive home.

He pulled into his driveway and muttered under his breath. The living room lights were on and his wife's car was in the driveway. He glanced back to the rearview mirror again, making sure the little girl didn't decide to make a break for it now that he stopped. Everything back there was calm. Not a peep or a grunt.

Inside, the house was bright and warm with the smell of rosemary wafting through the air. He took a deep breath and shook the rain off his jacket as he hung it by the door.

"Hello?" David called out.

"Oh, hi David," Bernice called out.

"Smells good."

"Well, it better. I've been working on this all day. Hungry?"

"Hi, dad!" Justine said.

Justine's tiny voice startled David as she ran past him and giggled. She was almost eight years old and smarter than David could have ever imagined a kid her age could be. He beamed with pride when he bragged about her scholastic achievements at work. Jared followed Justine, slapping David's leg as he walked by. Jared was almost five, and he didn't speak, despite Justine swearing that he spoke to her when they weren't around. Doctors gave him some sort of diagnosis, but it all felt like ways to make David pay more money for services they didn't need.

"Hey, kids," David called after them as they ran off through the house.

He joined Bernice in the kitchen, where she pulled a cooked and stuffed chicken from the oven and set it on the countertop.

"I thought you had plans with the kids tonight," David said.

"Well, we had plans but then the rain, and you know how Jared is in the rain."

"You should have told me. I could have come home sooner."

"Well, I didn't want to bother you. I did text you, though."

David glanced at his phone. The transaction screen he showed the seller was still pulled up. He closed it and checked his texts. Bernice was right. David's preoccupation with his purchase must have caused him to not notice his phone vibrate.

"You can't baby Jared," David said. "It's just a little rain."

"Don't start with me, David. Okay? It's been a rough day and I don't need this right now. Jared…"

"Okay, okay. I'm sorry. It smells great, Bernie."

They smiled and kissed.

"Jared is sensitive. You know that."

"I know, Bernie. I said I know."

"He doesn't like rain. It drives him nuts."

"I know, Bernie. I said that already."

"Set the table, get the kids to wash their hands."

"I would, but you know how Jared is with water," David said with a smile.

Bernice laughed and threw a kitchen towel at his head as he left the kitchen to hunt down his kids and get them ready for dinner.

Their forks clinked against the dishes. Justine yelled at Jared for eating "wrong." Bernice took breaks from her long, dull story to scold Justine. All their words and cries went ignored as David stared out the front window at his car in the driveway. There still had been no movement, but at any moment, the sedative could wear off and that little girl in his trunk could destroy his entire life.

"David? David, is everything alright?" Bernice asked.

"Yeah, Bernie. Sorry, my mind wandered for a bit."

"Busy day?"

"The usual. You know how Howard is this time of year."

Bernice took that as an excuse to launch into another long diatribe. Once again, David tuned her out and watched his car from the corner of his eye. He did not know how Howard was because David had called out to spend the day waiting in an abandoned parking lot for a stranger to drop off a little girl he bought online.

Dinner concluded, which led to chores and movie night. Then, at long last, he carried the kids from the couch to their beds, kissed Bernice on the forehead as she dozed off, and made his way downstairs. Bernie was a light sleeper, but he needed privacy. He took a little help from pills he found in the bathroom to make sure she stayed asleep a little sounder than usual that night. He grabbed a suitcase from the garage.

When he opened the trunk, the little girl still hadn't moved. Her chest rose and fell in a gentle rhythm, which assured him she was still alive. After checking for nosy neighbors, he laid the suitcase on the ground and lifted the girl into it. She was heavier than he imagined she would be.

He carried her to the house without a sound. Bernice snored upstairs, and the kids were in their rooms with their white noise machines running. He glanced back and saw something he had hoped not to see all night. This time, it was his fault. In his rush to get her inside before anyone woke up, he left the trunk open.

He stopped in the doorway to take a break and run back to close his trunk. A sprinkle of rain started again. He threw his arms over his head as if it would matter if he kept dry from a few splashes of water. He tiptoed out across the driveway and closed his trunk, careful not to slam it.

Then he tiptoed back inside. As he made his way into the doorway, he saw Jared playing with the zipper on the suitcase.

"Jared!" David hissed.

Jared snapped his hand away from the zipper and stepped back.

"What are you doing awake? It's past bedtime."

Jared stared at David and pointed at the suitcase. David's eyes followed where Jared pointed and he saw a sprout of black hair sticking out of the suitcase where Jared pulled the zipper down a few inches. He could see the hair, but nothing else.

"What is it, Jared?" David asked. Then he nodded as he said, "Is it a doll? Is it a doll, Jared?"

Jared shook his head and continued to point and grunt.

"It's a doll, alright. It's a gift for your sister. You don't want to spoil the surprise, right? It's a doll for Justine, Jared."

Jared smiled and covered his mouth with his hands as if to suppress his excitement at their shared secret. David tried not to roll his eyes. Eight sessions of intense, expensive therapy so Jared could learn emotional expression and all he gets is a cartoonish look of surprise. He was sure Jared understood nothing he was saying.

"That's right, Jared. Now, if you ruin the surprise, then I'll have to give this doll back, right? I can't give it to her anymore if it isn't a surprise. So let's keep this between us, alright?"

Jared nodded and stopped pointing, then slapped his father's leg. David and Bernie assumed it was Jared's form of a hug.

"Now go back to bed," David said. "We'll save this surprise for Christmas, alright?"

David brought the suitcase into the basement, then locked the door, in case Jared's curiosity about the doll grew. He made a mental note to find a life-size doll for Justine to open on Christmas.

The basement served as David's workspace and home office. His long career as a restoration architect taught him how to build strategically using existing materials and architectural style to expand upon a design. One of his favorite jobs was when a bar owner hired him to restore an old speakeasy for the historical society. In the course of his work, he discovered a hidden room that had not appeared on any of the blueprints. Whoever designed it all those decades ago used a series of mirrors to confuse an investigator who might suspect a hidden room. The mirrors, combined with an interlocking mechanism that required a piece to be put into place for the lock to work, inspired David. He took extensive notes and then dismantled the entry before showing his discovery to the owner. That room was so unique that he incorporated the hiding mechanism into the renovation of his basement. He didn't need police snooping around, learning about the mechanism from a bartender. It was a secret known only to him and the architect who built the place decades ago.

Among the rolled-up blueprints, architecture awards, and general clutter of the basement, there was an old mirror hung on the far wall. That mirror served as a piece of the intricate interlocking mechanism that David fiddled with to reveal a hidden room.

The soundproofing hid the screams from his family. Ventilation kept the occupant alive. He even wired the room in a way that only he could turn on the lights when it was open. This way, there was no chance that a forgotten light seeping through a microscopic crack could lead to the discovery of that room.

David pulled the girl from the suitcase and laid her down on a dirty mattress. It was Justine's from when she was a toddler.

"Can you hear me?" David asked.

The girl remained still except for her tiny chest, rising and falling with each breath. He brushed her dark, curled hair out of her face and admired her.

"Look, if you can hear me, I need you to know a few things. This is my house. I'm in charge here. What I say goes, understand? This room is soundproof. Scream all you want, claw at the walls, and do whatever you need to do to get it out of your system. You can't escape, and if you do, there's nowhere to go. I'll kill whoever tries to help you, even if it's my wife and kids. If you try to get their attention and they try to help you, their deaths will be on your head. Not mine. I'll give you a few days to get used to the room. I'll bring some food too every so often. You hear me?"

She remained quiet and still except for her breathing. He shrugged it off, closed the door, reset all the locks, and went to bed beside his wife.

The next day, he went home on his lunch break and brought food to the little girl. He made sure his wife was away doing groceries. The kids were at school. She was no longer lying still on the bed. She wasn't cowering in the corner or hiding or trying to run out either. Instead, she sat in the center of the room with her legs crossed and her hands rested on her lap. Her face had no expression and her eyes didn't move. David placed the food in front of her and stared back at her as she stared forward with no expression.

"Hey, you there?" David asked, waving his hand in front of her face.

She didn't blink.

"There's a bucket in the corner to shit in if you need to. There'll be more food later. If you want anything, need anything, you let me know, alright? I'm not a monster. You want crayons? Coloring books?"

He stared and waited for an answer, but she ignored him and remained still. Once again, he shrugged and closed the door, leaving her in complete darkness.

The next two days were the same. She sat in the center of the room, staring off at nothing. Then, on the third day, he brought her food yet again. This time, he took away the old food and placed the new plate in front of her. As he stepped back, her head snapped toward him. A slight smile crept across her face.

"So, there is someone in there?" He said, half joking. "You alright?"

She didn't reply or move again. She only stared and kept the half smile across her face as he left the room and locked her away in the darkness. He didn't know what to make of her. Perhaps she suffered from a mental illness. It could be nothing more than an adjustment period. He tried not to think about her being stolen away from her family or sold off for a junkie to get their fix.

The next day, he arrived home from work to the sounds of laughter and young children screaming and playing. Their tiny but mighty footsteps scampered around the house. He made his way through the living room, smiling at the sound of his daughter's giggle and the clapping of his son.

Then he heard another laugh he hadn't heard before.

His wife was in the kitchen with the news playing in the background. She chopped vegetables, preparing for dinner that night. He laid his lunchbox on the counter and wrapped an arm around his wife's neck, laying a gentle kiss on her cheek. Not that he loved her or felt even the slightest bit of affection for her. She had grown old and fat and her attitude worsened with each day. His good mood arose from knowing that tonight, he would finally use his recent purchase.

"They have a friend over?" He asked, his hand slipping away from around his wife.

"Some girl, I didn't catch her name. I guess from school, or maybe she moved in down the street. I saw that one on the corner sold. Maybe they have a kid?"

"Yeah, maybe. What's for —"

"Hi, Mr. Andrews," a little voice called out from behind David.

He turned with a smile to greet his daughter's new friend. As he turned, his face turned pale and an icy chill crept through his body.

"It can't be," he muttered to himself.

The little girl looked exactly like the little girl he had locked away in the basement. She had the same dark hair and a similar complexion. Even her clothes looked like the same clothes as the girl locked away downstairs. He stuttered a greeting back. She giggled and ran off to hide as his daughter counted out in the other room.

"Can't be what?" Bernice asked.

David turned back to her, still pale, as if he had seen a ghost.

"Are you alright?"

"Yeah, yes. I'm fine. That was…?"

"That's Justine and Jared's new little friend. Cute, right?"

"You know, maybe we should ask her where she lives. Her parents might be worried."

"I tried, but she kept assuring me it was alright and Justine backed her up. I guess they planned this earlier today."

"You think she lives where? The house you said that sold?"

"You know, the yellow one on the corner."

"Maybe I should see if —"

"Don't worry about it, honey. I already tried. We went for a walk earlier. No one was home. We'll try again after dinner. Go get washed up and set the table, yeah? Let the kids play."

"Sure, I need to run downstairs and check on something first. A project."

"Save it for later. The kids are hungry and you know how they can get."

"It'll just be a minute," David insisted.

"David. Please. Wash your hands and set the table. You spend so much time down there."

"It'll just be a minute," he called out, already down the hall.

His heart raced as his feet thundered down the stairs. He ran through the basement, to the false wall, threw the mechanism into place, yanked it open, and pulled open the door. Empty.

The little girl who had been so still the last few days was nowhere to be found, but in the place where she sat was a little blue bow. He hadn't noticed but assumed she had it pinned in her hair when he got her.

His heart continued to thunder. He could hear his pulse in his ears. He sealed everything up behind him and made his way back upstairs. As he stepped out from the basement, his daughter and her friend, his prisoner, scampered by, full of laughs.

"What is going on with you?" his wife asked. "Are you feeling sick? Maybe you should lie down? Skip dinner?"

"No, no. I'm fine," he said. "Just a long day. I'm starving. Let's eat."

Bernice disappeared to find the kids and make sure they washed their hands before dinner. David set the table, his ears ringing and face hot. His mind ran through all the possibilities, all the questions. She had been catatonic since he got her, yet there she was, running around and playing with his kids. How would he explain it? Was it a game, or was she too stupid to understand what was happening? Or is she smart? Was this her plan? What's her endgame?

His mind was so overclocked he didn't hear her walk in behind him until she pulled out the chair and took a seat at the head of the table. She had a big smile, a knowing one that was far from innocent. The other kids splashed around in the sink as Bernice shouted for them to hurry and to behave.

"That's my seat," he grumbled to the girl.

"What are you going to do about it, Mr. Andrews?"

"What is this? What are you doing here? You escaped. Run away. Go. Tell the police whatever you want."

"Why would I do that?"

"Well, what do you want?" He shouted.

Bernice turned the corner at the tail end of his words, the kids in tow. He tried to recover before she reacted.

"We have what, chicken? Potatoes, rice, broccoli? That's all good with you, right?"

"Everything sounds delicious. I'll take a little of each."

"Oh, honey, you're sitting in Mr. Andrews' seat," Bernice said. "Would you mind moving over next to Justine?"

"Bernice, it's fine. I told her to sit there. I'll sit between her and Justine."

"You sure?"

"It's not a problem at all."

They each took their seats and distributed the food amongst them. David couldn't help but monitor the girl. The sounds of their silverware tapping the plates filled the silence until Bernice spoke.

"So, where do you live, exactly?"

"I live nearby," the little girl said. "Very close by. I've only been there a few days, though."

"Yes, I understand, and we love having you here, but I'm sure your mother is worried about where you might be. Do you mind telling me how I can get hold of her? I want to let her know you're here. You know, so she can pick you up, or we can drop you off."

"I thought I lived here," the girl said, looking at David.

"I'm sorry. Justine didn't check with us on that," Bernice said with a laugh, thinking little of it.

David moved his eyes to the food on his plate and shoved some into his mouth. He needed a way out, and it seemed like the only way was to kill her. He needed to get her away from his family, then he could do it. Slit her throat? No, something bloodless. He settled on strangling her when no one was watching, then locking her back up in the basement. He could excuse her absence as her having gone home without telling them. But then Bernice's nosiness handed him the opportunity he needed.

"I can drop you off after dinner," David said.

The two locked eyes, each playing with the other person, neither knowing the other's endgame. Well, he didn't know hers, and she sure knew his. She smiled, quick-chewed her food, and swallowed it with a nod.

"Oh," she said. "That would be great, but unnecessary. See, I live here, in the basement. In that little room you built into the wall downstairs, outside of your work area."

David froze. His grip around his steak knife tightened as he narrowed his eyes. He could excuse it away to Bernice, but he needed the girl dead and gone and right then and right there before she exposed any more of his double life.

Even the slightest suspicion could unravel and destroy everything.

"I'm sorry?" Bernice said from across the table.

"Yeah, I live..."

"She's joking, Bernie. I told her I had a lot of space downstairs. I guess she thought I was inviting her to stay there. No, honey. I'm sorry. Your parents are probably worried sick about you. How about we head out right now before it gets too late?"

"I don't have anywhere to go," she said. "I'm your property now, David. Remember? That's why you bought me."

"Okay, young lady," Bernice said. "We don't play games like that in this house. I think it's time you leave."

"I told you, Bernice, I can't leave. I live here. Downstairs. Right, David? Tell her."

"That's it," David roared, slamming his fist into the table. "Let's go."

His voice sent a shockwave through the dining room. His kids trembled and their eyes went wide. Tears pooled and spilled down their cheeks. They had never seen their father act this way before, and Bernice never knew David to have an angry bone in his body. She, too, trembled at his thundering voice.

The little girl pushed herself back in her chair, but she didn't stand up. Instead, she smiled at David and spoke.

"You told me that if I alerted your family, if they found out about me, about your little playroom downstairs, you'd kill them."

"This is too much," Bernice said, wiping her mouth and finally relinquishing her fork to her plate. "Kids, go to your room. I don't know what this is about, if it's a prank or for..."

"Have you ever been downstairs?" the girl asked.

"Let's go," David said, standing and reaching for the girl's arm.

"Don't you wonder what happened to that little girl from church?"

Bernice turned pale.

"Don't you dare," Bernice said. "That little girl will not be part of this cruel joke."

"I got this, Bernie. Kids, your mother said to go to your rooms. Go. Now. Bernie, why don't you go too? I'll make sure she gets home."

"Don't leave me alone with him," the girl said, forcing a quiver in her voice, making herself small. Bernie froze and looked between the two of them. "Does he ever let you down there?"

"No," Bernie said, her voice faltering.

"Bernie..."

"Where'd they find the girl from your church?" the girl asked.

"Along Calaveras, by the on-ramp. Someone tossed her while they drove off," Bernie said.

"Which ramp?"

"880 South."

"What route does David take to work?"

"Calaveras, to 880 south."

"And you've never seen the basement?"

"Not for a long time."

"Bernie, take the kids upstairs."

"I told them, David," the girl said. "Are you going to do it?"

Bernie looked at the girl, the last shred of her disbelief dangling, about to fall. David glanced back and forth between them, not answering the girl. Not saying no.

"Are you going to kill them?" The girl asked, determined to get an answer.

"Kids," Bernie said, taking a step away from David. "Go upstairs and lock your doors. Now."

The kids got up to head upstairs but as they passed their father; he grabbed Justine's tiny bicep and told her to wait. With his other hand, he toyed with the steak knife.

"David?" Bernie called to him.

Still, he didn't reply. He adjusted his grip on his knife and held his daughter's arm tighter, pulling her closer to him. Bernie crossed the room and put her hand on David's shoulder.

"Let go of our daughter, David. Tell me what's going on. What's in the basement? Who is this girl?"

"Bernie, Bernie, Bernie. I'm tired. Tired of everything. Your overbearing nature, your age, and the wrinkles every year has brought to your fat ass. And the kids. These fucking kids. They are always asking for everything. New toys, new clothes. I give you all everything that I can give you and yet, I can't get a little indiscretion for me doing something I love. Sit down, kids. And you. What do you want? You want me to kill them?"

"No," the little girl said. "Not quite."

"Then what?"

"I want you to finish your dinner."

"Why is that?"

"The drugs don't seem to work."

David looked down at his plate, then back at the girl. After a moment of contemplation, he swept his hand across the table, sending the plate flying against the wall. It shattered to pieces. He grabbed his cup and threw it across the table. Bernie jumped up from her chair moments before the cup slammed into it.

"David!" Bernie shouted. "Kids, run. Now!"

Justine pulled out of her father's grasp, grabbed Jared's hand, and ran out of the dining room with him. The little girl followed, but stopped at the bottom of the stairs, watching the drama unfold on her behalf. Bernie nodded to her, letting her know she was safe and should wait upstairs. She did as they planned and went upstairs until the noise settled.

***

Thirty years after that fateful dinner, Justine and her husband, Ignacio, sat at that same dinner table. She poked the food on her plate around as she stared at it. Her appetite hadn't been what it once was since the kids moved out. Sarah had moved on to marry a doctor and moved in with him at his mansion in the hills. Brock finished trade school and moved in with his pregnant girlfriend. She hoped they would be married before the baby came, but she dared not pry for the sake of her son. The absence that hurt the most was Jared's. His condition worsened after their father left. By the time they reached adulthood, it became a fight to get him to leave the house. So he stayed with them and became best friends with Ignacio until he died. Too young, yet his death also brought a wave of relief to the family. Though none of them would admit it.

Ignacio meant the world to her. He taught her how men should act. Never did he complain about Jared being around as they raised their family; he loved him like his own brother. He gave Justine everything and anything she could ever want.

She would have to try quite hard to find a single thing he had ever done to hurt her. And yet, the one thing he asked for was something she wasn't sure if she could give him.

"What's on your mind?" Ignacio asked from across the table.

"We can do it," Justine said. "Let's sell the house."

A smile spread across his lips, and he ran around the table and wrapped his arms around her. A wet kiss warmed her forehead.

"You sure?"

"Yes, but…"

"I know. It'll be hard. You grew up here. I get it. But this job pays twice as much. The kids are all out of the house. We can get some good money for this place."

"No, I know. I understand. But there's something I need to tell you. You can never mention this to another person and we may need to do something terrible. But it'll be worth it, I swear."

Ignacio's arm fell off Justine's shoulders. He slid into the chair next to her with concern painted across his face.

"You're scaring me. What's going on? You can tell me anything. I swear. You know that."

"I know."

"So, what is it? Whatever it is, we'll figure it out."

"We used to play hide and seek," Justine said. "One day, I hid down in the basement, knowing my brother would be too scared to look. I'd finally win. But as I hid, my father came down. I knew I wasn't supposed to be there, so I stayed quiet and moved further into my hiding spot. It was in the corner, next to the couch. I saw him open the wall and walk inside. He was in there for a few minutes, then he came back out with a smile on his face. Closed the wall behind him. I was a kid. I didn't know what to make of it. We knew never to go down there, but I was rebellious enough not to fear him. Of course, that was before I knew everything.

"The next day, Jared told me he saw my dad with a doll in a suitcase and it was tall and pretty and had beautiful hair. Jared told me he took it down to the basement to hide for my Christmas gift. I knew something was off about what he said, and that room, that hidden room, was fresh in my mind. So, the next morning, my dad went to work. I snuck downstairs, opened the wall, and…there was a little girl there. She didn't move at first, but when I said hello to her, she heard my voice and sat up. She told me to run, that he'd hurt me for talking to her. I told her she could run and leave and call the cops. She was too scared that he might hurt us if she escaped because the only way for her to get out was if someone let her out. She was a little older than me, I think. But she said she didn't know where to go. Her parents sold her to one of her mother's friends. People shipped her around, starved her, and beat her. When she ended up there, she was so emaciated it stunted her growth and made her look younger than she was. She told me she was twelve.

"She made me promise not to tell my mother, but I knew it was wrong. I don't think I understood it, but I knew that whatever that was, was wrong. So, I told my mom. She was in denial at first, but once I dragged her down there and showed her, she found out what kind of man my father was. From that moment on, my father wasn't my father. He was a monster. All these strange things about him were finally making sense. I knew then, she assured me and even now, looking back, I know she was right. One day, me or my brother, or both of us, would become his victims. So, we let the girl out one day when he was gone and played it casual, letting her be our friend, and join us for dinner. It was my mom's plan. It took me a long time to understand it, but I get it now."

"Jesus Christ. I thought your father left one day and never came back," Ignacio said. "Where is this story going?"

"Can I show you? In the basement?"

"The room is still there?"

"I think the story would be better if I showed you."

She led Ignacio down those stairs. For the last thirty years, she had been too scared to go down there. She only did so on rare occasions and only for good reason. In the basement, she crossed the room and inserted a lever beneath the mirror that hung on the wall. She took a moment to breathe. Once she activated the wall to open, there would be no turning back. Whatever she saw hidden away on the other side would be a confirmation of everything she had gone through in life. Tears welled in her eyes and in that moment, more than ever, she missed her brother. If she could hold his hand in that moment, she knew she'd be stronger. The reality of it all had grown into a heavy pit, seated deep in her gut. Opening the room would be the first step in doing what she knew needed to be done. She looked over at Ignacio, who deserved the truth and everything he ever wanted. For him, she pulled the lever.

The wall cracked open, and the smell of stale, dry air filled the basement. Justine pushed the wall and slid it aside. She stepped in and activated the lights, revealing the skeletal remains of her dead father lying in the middle of the room. Ignacio stepped in and took in the sight of it with wide eyes and a lack of words to say. He ran his hands through his hair, glancing back and forth between Justine and the skeleton.

"Ignacio, meet my father," Justine said, gesturing at it. "My mom put something in his food that day. Drugged him. During their argument, it took hold and brought him down. She carried him into the basement and locked him up in the room. When his work called to report him as a no-show the next day, we reported him missing. Made it look like he left us and disappeared."

"And the whole time he was down here? Did you feed him?"

"Nope. I didn't know everything that happened. After we went upstairs during dinner, we hid in the room, crying. Eventually, my mom came and got us. She said he left. I asked more questions as I got older. When she thought I was old enough, my mom told me everything. A few years after we reported him missing, we got a payout from his insurance. Sold his shit. It put me through college. Anyway, if we sell the house, we need to get rid of the body. Destroy this room, or seal it away forever."

Ignacio stood and looked around the room. He ran his finger over the scratch marks on the walls. He checked the bucket in the corner. Someone had used it, but it dried up. Even the mattress has deteriorated. However, the lack of bugs and airflow mummified the remains.

"What happened to the little girl?"

"I don't know. My mom told me she asked for bus fare. She had a brother somewhere, and she wanted to find him. We never heard from her again."

"How do we get rid of him?" Ignacio asked.

"No idea," Justine admitted.

They stood in the room, staring down at the twisted face of her dead father's mummified corpse, trying to come up with a way to turn him to dust so he would never burden them again.

| 19 |

DINNER

The soup was delicious, but I wish someone had told me he was a cannibal when I received the invitation. I would have brought dessert.

| 20 |

THAT OLD HOUSE

The following is an epistolary story (a story written as letters) and so this page is, other than the title and this description, intentionally blank to allow the formatting room to breathe.

To whom it may concern,

I hope this letter finds you well.

I came across the listing for this house and saw that someone recently transferred ownership to a new owner, who I assume is you. Forgive my not leaving a name and only a PO BOX as a return address, I would rather remain anonymous.

My reason for reaching out today is that I lived there as a child. I have many glorious memories of that old house. I remember learning to ride my bike, reading books beneath the trees in the backyard.

They're quite wonderful memories, but more than not, I have nightmares of that old house. I do not intend to scare you, but I can't help but wonder...

Have you heard the scratching on the walls?

Regards,
Curious

Dear Curious,

Thank you for the well wishes.

I inherited the property from my father, who passed away three months back. I hadn't realized he owned this old house until a lawyer showed up on my doorstep with a will (which I also didn't know he had).

It seems he bought the old house but never lived in it. With your letter, I can't help but admit that you have piqued my curiosity.

Scratching on the walls?

I wonder if this is why he never lived in that old house...

Sincerely,
HomeOwner

Dear HomeOwner,

Thank you for the prompt reply and for humoring my question.

That old house has changed hands many times and too often my letters go unanswered for one reason or another.

I say "humoring" my question, but I mean it with all sincerity. Something is inside that house. I caution you to steer clear for your own sanity and well being. The fact that you are receiving these notes means you have been to the property.

Can you feel it? I'm sure you can. There is something in the air on that land. It is thick, hard to breathe. The floors creak with each step, the attic is cold and damp, and, as I said, something scratches at the walls. Not all the time, not every day, not every night. The sounds often come late when nothing is stirring, no sounds to be heard but your own frantic breath as the scratches grow louder.

Please, I wonder, have you yet heard the scratching on the walls?

Regards,
Curious

Dear Curious,

I apologize for the delay in my response. I have been quite busy with my father's estate.

To tell you the truth, I have not yet come across anything that might be a key to that old house and so I have not made my way inside, though I have looked through the windows. I've not seen anything odd but, it is eerie to stare into an empty house.

As I searched through my father's old things, I found something that might interest you. He kept a journal (yet another surprise). In his journal there was an entry which I've transcribed below:

I bought a house! It had been on the market for so long, they reduced the price a dozen times. It's small and old but I think we can make it work. There's a barn in the driveway. It leans to the right, and it's filled with hay and old horse shoes, but I think I can make a garage out of it, or maybe a workshop for future projects. I wonder how old the large pine trees in the backyard are. It's such an enormous space, we may even get a dog.

My mom died shortly after this entry, so it seems they never had the chance to live there. I must admit, without her as the glue, we rarely spoke to my father in his last few years so he hadn't told me anything.

Sorry to bother you with my family drama. To be honest, it feels good to speak to a stranger about this, but I won't burden you any further.

Sincerely,
HomeOwner

P.S. After writing this, but before I had the chance to send it, I read the last entry in his journal. It speaks for itself, so I'll leave you with his words...

I thought this old house would be a welcome distraction. I miss my wife. She would have loved everything about it... maybe not everything.

I lost track of time today and fell asleep after working on the plumbing in the bathroom. I woke late at night and I could have sworn I heard something scratching on the wall behind where I leaned my head... I'm sure it's nothing. Rats maybe.

Dear HomeOwner,

I am sorry to hear about your loss. Death is never easy. My best to you and your family. I, too, know the struggles of alienation and sadness. Some of it was unavoidable, and some of it, I blame on the house.

Thank you for sharing the entries from your father's journal. Have you found anything else written?

Please, even if you find the key, do not go into that house. It may be safe the first time or the first dozen, but once you hear the scratching at the walls... it only gets worse from there.

You sound like a kind person. Sell it now, while you can. If not, maybe even consider burning it to the ground.

Regards,
Curious

D ear Curious,

Thank you for the well wishes. Our mother's death was easier because we knew it was better than the pain she dealt with every day, even so, thank you.

I know you warn me of that old house, but I am not sure how you expect me to deal with it. It is a house, after all. Our own home is quite small with noisy neighbors. An escape to the country would be welcome. My wife and I have discussed potentially moving into the house.

I do have some skepticism about your warnings. I would rather confirm it for myself. With that said, I now realize I have no way of knowing if you are a prankster with too much time on your hands or if you have some mental deficiency, especially considering the last part of your previous communication. I will not burn the house down because of the whims of a stranger.

Please tell me your name and prove to me you once lived in that old house, and maybe I'll humor you further. I don't mean to be rude, but I also refuse to be a fool.

I wish you the best. Please send no further correspondence if you're unable to prove your claims. If I decide I believe you, I will reach out.

Sincerely,
HomeOwner

P.S. I've not found any other evidence of "scratching on the wall" among my father's writings.

Dear HomeOwner,

Unfortunately, I cannot reveal my identity. I am a private person, struggling to get through each day because of what I went through in that old house. I only wish to warn you. Perhaps one day you will understand why.

Regardless, I wish you the best. I remain available should you choose to continue these letters.

I can only warn you so much to not enter that cursed old house. If you move in and experience nothing of the sort that I've experienced there as a child, I will be ecstatic. There is a room by the back entrance. The walls are painted blue, not by me but by a tenant before you. If you go into the closet, you can remove a small panel of wood from the back wall. Behind that panel lies a torn page from an old Playboy magazine that I stashed away as a child. That's my proof, although another curious young boy could have discovered it already.

I wish you the best.

Regards,
Curious

D^{ear Curious,}

My sincerest apologies for any doubts and for taking so long to write back.

I will not waste time. I entered that old house.

The floors creak. It smells of mold. The windows stick. Someone tore up the carpets and never replaced them. There is an uncomfortable feeling in the pantry off from the kitchen I cannot describe.

You were right about the blue room and the panel of wood, though I found no Playboy excerpt hidden inside. Either way, I believe you. Not only because of the hidden panel...

I heard scratching on the wall.

I was replacing a broken door and took a break. I leaned against the wall as I drank water. Just behind me, something scratched at the wall. Just as my father described. It sounded like an animal trying to escape, but there was something about the way the sound moved... It sounded intentional and not like the scrambling of a desperate rat.

Please, tell me about the scratching on the wall. Tell me everything about that old house.

Sincerely,
HomeOwner

D ear HomeOwner,

I am both glad and saddened to hear from you again.

After not hearing from you for several weeks, I hoped you had no experiences and would live happily ever after. I'm sorry to see that is not the case. Has your family moved in yet? I hope not. If so, they should leave immediately. For you, it may be too late.

I can't remember the first time my siblings and I heard the scratches on the wall. We heard it so often they all blend in my memory.

My parents would tell us rats lived in the walls and they were crawling, skittering their little claws against the wood of the wall. I believed it. That's why we had a cat.

I stopped believing them when I found the cat's body.

After she died, we heard her meowing to be let in. We'd run to the door, or to the window to look for her. Maybe it was all a dream, and she was safe and alive, we thought. We'd swing open the door, but there'd be nothing there.

Her meows haunt me as much as the scratches.

One night I heard a scratch at my window. My fear prevented me from opening the blinds. The scratch dragged across the wall. I couldn't help but follow it. I followed it as best I could around the house and through the kitchen and dining room and into the living room. As it scratched along that living room wall, I noticed an open window. I froze, wondering what would happen if the scratching noise passed that open window. I was determined to see what it was at last. It got closer and closer. Just as it reached that open window, I ducked. I was too terrified to look. It stopped. I held my breath, imagining some horrific face staring in and searching for me. After a few moments, the scratching continued. It dragged along the rest of the house and back to my window, where it stopped. Many sleepless nights followed.

Stay out of the cellar if you hear screams.

Regards,
Curious

D ear Curious,

What is this house? Although I sent my family away, something pulls me back. I am obsessed. I hear the scratching more now. Not always. Some nights are quiet. I heard your cat as well. She seems to have friends now. I leave cat food outside. I think it's a sympathetic gesture, even if they can't eat it. How long ago did you leave? I have heard the scratch dragging along the wall. I want to leave the windows open to see what scratches at night, but like you were all those years ago, I am also terrified of finding out. What if it's something much worse than I could imagine?

I pulled into the driveway one afternoon. As I did, I saw a face watching from the window of the back entrance. The blue room where you once slept. I raced inside and scoured the house but found no one.

Have you seen her before?

Sincerely,
HomeOwner

D ear HomeOwner,

I am so very sorry for my delayed response.

I have fallen into a depressive state. These memories are flooding back to me, and are so vivid, it's as if I never left that house. I'm better now. I am working with a psychiatrist and I have increased my prescription. She suggests I stop writing to you. She thinks I am lying about someone writing me back. I showed her the letters, but she has suspicions I am typing to myself. I don't think she will ever believe me, so I will have to keep our communication a secret as my medications align.

Yes, there was a girl. I once saw her playing with my toys out in the yard. I joined her until we played a game of hide and seek. She insisted I hide in the basement. When I went down there, I turned around and she was gone; the door locked behind me. My mother told me to never speak to her again. I would see her playing outside sometimes. She seemed lonely. My mother would pull the curtains shut tight if she ever saw her out there.

I wish I could ask my parents about that old house, but they've both long since passed. Years after moving out, I confronted my mother about my memories of that place. She couldn't remember any of what I said. She didn't remember the "rats in the walls" as she called it, or the little girl outside.

If you hear the girl calling you for help, do not go. Trust me. Listen to me. I beg of you. Let her scream until she stops. Also, be cautious, she is not the one who scratches at the wall.

Regards,
Curious

P.S. Stop feeding the cats.

Dear HomeOwner,

I have not heard from you for several weeks.

I hope you have sent no desperate letters that were lost in the mail.

Are you alright?

Should we forego the snail mail and speak directly? Though I need my privacy, for your sake and the sake of your family, I will be more direct. I want to help you!

Please let me know your thoughts.

Regards,
Curious

D ear HomeOwner,

I haven't heard from you for months.

I can't help but assume the worst. If you are safe, write
back.

Please.

Regards,
Curious

Dear HomeOwner,

It has been a year, and I see the house once again listed for sale.

Please enlighten me, as I am curious about what happened. Are you still there? Have you stopped answering for some other reason? I am sorry to bother you but I am so curious, hence the penpal name.

Regards,
Curious

Dear Curious,

I received your letter in the envelope addressed to "Current Occupant," I hope it's okay that I reply. It seems you were in correspondence with the previous owner.

I just purchased this house from his estate. I'm sorry to inform you that the local police department declared him dead. Missing and never found after having a mental health episode. It was quite tragic and I hope his family has recovered and is doing well wherever they went.

I'm very sorry to share the news with you and I wish you all the best.

Sincerely,
The New Homeowner

D ear The New Homeowner,

Thank you for the update on my former penpal. I hope this letter finds you well.

Forgive my not leaving a name and a PO BOX as a return address, I would rather remain anonymous.

I lived there as a child. Although I have many fond memories of that old house, nightmares are what I remember most. I do not intend to scare you, but I can't help but wonder...

Have you heard the scratching on the walls?

Regards,
Curious

| 21 |

MUSH

The mushy meal melts in my mouth as I masticate meticulously. Macabre, maybe, malicious even, but I moan at the taste of the mourning Mr. Manson's mother's minced and marinated midbrain.

| 22 |

THE OFFICE DOWN THE HALL

The raucous party had dwindled to the final board members and a handful of yes-men with desperate hopes of making their way into the boys' club. And female companions. In the office at the end of the hall sat CEO Davis Kilpatrick and his attorney, Cleopatra. She was an unassuming young woman and a hell of a lawyer who knew better than to acknowledge the female companions. Only a dim light from a reading lamp on the desk lit the room.

Alcohol flowed, conversations murmured on, celebrating the victory they didn't deserve. Cheers and haughty laughter traveled down the hall to where Davis stared out the window, running his finger over the cover of his wet bar. Cleopatra completed the last few documents from their recent win, organized to ease the signing process. She pushed the papers forward and laid a pen on the paper next to where she had just drawn an "X" for him to sign.

"You're lucky," Cleopatra said.

"I'm lucky? I thought you were that great of a lawyer," David said, his words slurring into one another like bumper cars.

"No one is that great of a lawyer, Mr. Kilpatrick," Cleopatra said. She kept her arms crossed and eyes stern. Davis poured another two fingers of bourbon into a cup and sloshed it around as he stared at it.

"Well, either way, it's done now," he said.

"It is. For now, but I don't want to remind you again. I don't specialize in that area of law. I manage corporate takeovers, not sexual assault allegations."

"You're the best lawyer they have. You should feel flattered."

"I don't need to be flattered. I'm happy with what I do."

"You won the trial of a lifetime. I'm sure your partners will heave a hefty bonus in your direction. Whatever it is, I'll ask them to double it. I have the power to do that, you know."

"That isn't the point, Mr. Kilpatrick."

"Money is always the point. Drop a stack of money in the middle of upstanding, hard-working men, and within seconds, they become as barbarous as their ancestors fighting over a cave's warmth and a sabertooth's skin."

"I only stepped in to clear it up, to salvage this acquisition, which, by the way, is still far from finished."

"Yes, but with this little snafu out of the way, we're golden."

"Maybe."

Davis turned toward her and stumbled over to his desk, collapsing into the rich leather upholstery with a deep sigh.

He downed the rest of his drink, then slammed his empty cup on the mahogany desk beside the papers awaiting his signature.

"All I need to do is put my name right here, on this little old line, and everything goes away?"

"And the wire transfer," Cleopatra reminded him, knowing full well she'd spend the next week chasing him down to do that.

"How much is it again?"

"A lot. We'll review the numbers when it's time to make the transfer, but you're getting the deal of a lifetime."

"All because of her mother's cancer diagnosis..."

Davis eyed Cleopatra with suspicion.

"I'm sorry. Do you think I gave her mother cancer?"

"No, I don't. I mean, there has to be something else, right?"

"That money will go a long way to making her mother comfortable during her treatments. Sign the papers, Mr. Kilpatrick, and we can put all this behind us."

"How many?" he asked.

"I'm sorry?"

"The original case. How many of us had our names mentioned? I know I was, right? Ted? Zane? Bill?"

"I really should go if I want to file these papers early tomorrow."

"C'mon, the case is over. I know they instructed you to protect us from each other, but really, can't we move on now? How many? Who?"

Davis stood up and walked around his desk, sitting against the other side of it, looking directly down at Cleopatra.

"Fine, I'll go home and get some rest. I'll be in for them first thing in the morning. With signatures."

Cleopatra stood to leave, but Davis grabbed her arm and pulled her hard. She collapsed back into her chair. Before she had the chance to yell, to scream at him for touching her that way, he shuffled back over to the papers and had the pen in his hand, moving a letter opener out of the way.

"Yeah, yeah. I'll sign your papers."

"Thank you," Cleopatra said, her voice uneasy, but steadfast.

Dealing with people like him was nothing new to her. The world of corporate domination saw a million leaders like him rise and fall every day. She could stand up for herself when the time was right. Davis had never been inappropriate to her before. Considering the amount of money on the line and the time she spent working the case, she dismissed the arm grab. He had been drinking; he wasn't in control of himself. At least he was singing the papers. She'd be in her car, driving home, and this would all be in the past.

Or so she thought. Then he opened his mouth and spoke, and she knew it wasn't an accident.

"You're an exquisite woman," he said.

"Just sign the papers, Mr. Kilpatrick."

"Did you hear me?"

"Thank you, but I have to be going."

He scribbled the last few signatures, then shoved them into the manilla folder and held them out for her. She stood and reached for them, but, as she expected, he pulled them away at the last second.

These men were all the same. They all thought they were the champions of the world, but they were only the champions of their little bubbles. People around them wanted their money or power. Whenever they met a woman who saw through that, they grew frustrated. They didn't know how to take "no" for an answer. They all made the same moves as if there was a class for corporate assholes and they all learned from the same teacher. More times than she cared to remember, she had experienced files being pulled away from her at the last second. A snarky smile and the cheap stench of arrogance often followed.

"Let's not do this," Cleopatra said.

"Do what? Sign the papers? You've been asking me to do that all night."

"You know what I mean."

"They're right here," he said, holding them close to himself, knowing that to take them from him, she'd have to step in close enough for him to smell her.

She stared at him and decided if it was worth fighting him over, or if she could walk away and collect the papers another day. She nodded and grabbed her purse.

"I'll be back to get them in the morning," she said, heading toward the door.

"Cleopatra. What a name. You're a lot like her too. Beautiful. Powerful. Strong-willed. Exotic."

"This is incredibly inappropriate," she said. At the door, she stopped and peered out through the glass. She saw his board members, all of whom were his minions, resembling and behaving like him, with the aspiration of becoming him one day. She rolled her eyes and pulled the door open. It was abruptly slammed shut by his hand. She stepped back, eyes wide and hands clutching her keys. She didn't want him to see her frazzled, but he was too close, too fast for her to pretend he wasn't terrifying her. He held up the papers.

"I bet men have gone to war for you throughout your life."

"I've heard all this before," she said. "You're lucky we have this merger to get through or I'd be at the courthouse first thing tomorrow filing a lawsuit of my own. Now step back and let me leave."

She snatched the documents from his hand and crossed her arms, waiting for him to move away from the door. She tapped her finger against her elbow to steady herself. The last thing she wanted was for him to see her tremble. No matter how pathetic a hungry lion might be, they're still natural predators with weight and strength on their side. The prey has to look strong or develop the skills necessary to fool the lions long enough to get to safety.

"You're right," he said, squeezing his eyes, then rubbing his temples. "I'm sorry. Please, have a seat. I don't mean to come off this way."

"I'll leave, thank you."

"I wasn't asking."

"I don't take orders from you."

"She was a goddess on Earth, Cleopatra. The odds defied the logic of her existence. Inbred, and yet, among those genetic monstrosities, a queen who can bed any man she set eyes on. Like the real Cleopatra, you could have men like me wrapped around your fingers."

"Men like you?" She asked, knowing better than to engage but unable to stop herself.

"Why settle for anything less than a king?"

"A king? For centuries kings have taken women by force, using not their charm or good looks, but their money and power because they were too pathetic to pick up a woman through their inferior wit. Let's skip the romance and you can play the part of King Louis XVI. Maybe one of your friends out there has a nice, shiny guillotine ready and waiting."

"You ungrateful whore."

Cleopatra slapped Davis across the face. She was more stunned than him. In that frozen moment of panic, wondering if she had really done that, he stomped toward her and grabbed her. He dragged her by the arm over to the chair at his desk and threw her into it again. Her body slammed against it with enough force that the front legs lifted off the ground for a moment, then crashed back down onto the floor.

"I'm going to ruin your career. How dare you slap me?"

"I didn't have a choice. Don't you ever lay a hand on me. I'm leaving."

He sat at his desk and fumbled around for something. She rose from the chair and looked down at the papers in her hand. Devious thoughts ran through her mind. It would be much easier for her to drop them in a shredder than it would be for her to make her way down to the courthouse the next day.

Before she had the chance to decide or to take another step, she heard an all-too-familiar sound, the click-clack of a gun being racked.

Her heart leaped into her throat. She turned, wishing it all to go away, for what she thought she heard, to not be real. Yet, when she turned, it confirmed her greatest fear. Davis had a cocked gun, sitting on the desk in front of him. The barrel faced her. He stared at her. Glared. Dark shadows crossed his face. His hand rested on the gun. His finger toyed with the trigger as if feeling it for the first time and imagining the power it could unleash.

"This has gone far enough," she choked out.

"You don't make the demands here."

The silence thickened as the two stared each other down. One, an unrelenting force who had built a reputation for remaining steadfast against anyone who got in their way. The other, a narcissist with alcohol on his breath and a loaded gun on his desk. An equally unrelenting force, facing her down and showing the sharpness of his teeth. Neither flinched nor blinked. They stared into each other's souls without a trace of emotion, both unwilling or unable to relent. She refused to give in to him, to let him have any ounce of power over her, but the stare of the gun kept her heart pounding away in her chest. She struggled to focus on her options, seeing only one. He knew he had her in more ways than she could ever know. Then, finally, he said words that turned her blood into fire.

"I raped someone once," he said.

Those evil words hung in the hair, balanced on the tension in the room. Tears streamed down Cleopatra's cheeks, yet she didn't weep, didn't blink. She stared and let her hands tremble.

"Why would you... why would you tell me that?"

"She was young. I was younger too."

She gripped the papers tight as if they offered protection.

"I was at a lake," Davis continued. "Sixteen years old. Athletic. Lacrosse. Spent every weekend at my dad's lake house out in Rhode Island. One summer, I was on the beach, going for an early walk. I had broken up with my girlfriend a few nights before. So there I was at the beach, and there was this girl. Couldn't have been more than a few years younger than me, and she was heading into the bathroom. I remember her as clear as day. She had this backpack with—"

"—Backpack," Cleopatra interjected. "She had a backpack with a keychain on it, a Guardian Man keychain. You... you followed her into the stall. Grabbed her. Put your hand over her mouth and you... you..."

"There it is. We worked side by side for months and you never even looked at me like you suspected. You didn't know? I recognized you right away. You were the first girl I ever fucked."

"You didn't fuck me... you raped me."

She wanted to scream the words so loud that they shattered all the windows in the office but they came out as a whimper.

"Oh, the pussy. It was so good. I couldn't get it out of my mind. Even when I got older. I dated women, beautiful women, supermodels, the most expensive whores in America, and yet, nothing compares to you. Nothing compared to that first fuck in that bathroom stall on the lake in Rhode Island."

She went to therapy, took drugs, self-medicated, self-harmed. She went through the darkest pits of Hell to run away from that memory, but all she ever saw and smelled and felt when she closed her eyes was that disgusting person in the bathroom stall. His sweaty hand wrapped around her mouth and then…

"Oh, I've hunted that same sensation across the world. Did you know that in Thailand, in the Philippines, and all around the world, you can just pay and have little virgin girls brought to you? I tried to find one to match, but every single one of them, every time… they weren't the same. There was something about you I couldn't get out of my head. And so, we escalated things. Oh, oops. I said "we" didn't I? The boys, the ones out there hooting and hollering? They became part of my group. They helped me find what I was looking for here and abroad.

It grew to be a competition. For them, it was fun and games. I'd dismiss a girl, then they'd take their turns with her. Recently though, that lawsuit in your hands? That's when things got out of hand. We did those things, everything they said, whatever they said, we did it. We turned that girl into a drugged-up sex doll, ready and eager to do whatever we wanted, but you know what? It wasn't right. It was close, but there's nothing like the original. No matter how new, how fresh, the original is always the best."

"You're fucking sick," Cleopatra spat out. "I want to leave. Right now."

His hand inched closer to holding the gun like a good and proper murder weapon. He said nothing in response, just smiled a sinister smile that stretched his eyes back.

"I've searched the entire world to find you again. When you showed up that day, I thought, 'No, it couldn't be her, could it? Would the universe drop her into my lap like that?' I called friends, found a copy of the police report, and sure enough, it was you. Cleopatra, a name so fitting for such an elusive girl."

"I was a child. You ruined my life."

"You seem to do pretty well for yourself."

"That isn't what I mean, and you know it. I know you know it, deep down inside you somewhere. You know you're a fucking monster."

"I know it. I know it right on the fucking surface. See, it's that killer instinct, that refusal to settle, that brought me to the top of the fucking world. That ambition drove me and still drives me and will continue to drive me until the day I die. That ambition is something you lack. You did nothing in this case. I could have had a dozen lawyers at the ready. They were banging down my door for a chance to defend me and build their names on the footprints of my empire. Instead, I gave you the chance. I needed you close to me. I needed to see what I created when I took you to that bathroom."

"And?"

"And I wasn't happy. I wanted a pathetic little girl who whimpered when I went inside her. Instead, I have this confident bitch standing in front of me with her three-piece suit and good posture. I wanted a broken girl who needed me as much as I needed her."

"You're angry I didn't let you define me?"

"I'm angry that you didn't scour the world trying to find me to let me do it to you again. You aren't on your knees begging me for another taste. I'm going to have to take it again, aren't I? Maybe that will make up for the years of searching. Breaking this confident whore in front of me will be worthwhile. I can feel it in my bones."

Cleopatra shook her head as the tears continued to roll down her cheeks. She had imagined a confrontation like this every night since that incident. She always wanted the chance to confront her attacker, make him pay, and make him feel pathetic. He was right. He was on top of the world, and she couldn't touch him. She wanted to get as far away from him as possible. Her father never looked at her the same, never looked at himself the same. Her mother said that he always regretted not being able to protect her, or not strengthening her to fight back to protect herself. Yet, there she was, decades later, in the same situation and still feeling like a child. She wanted nothing more than to give her father a second chance and have him barge through those doors, rip the gun from Davis' hands, and fill him with his own bullets. That could never happen. She and her father grew apart. He died after a battle with cancer, never knowing who hurt his baby girl and never holding her again, letting her know she was safe. Because she wasn't. He could never make that promise to her again. She was never safe.

She looked Davis in the eyes and saw every horrible thing looking back at her. Her eyes crawled to the gun on the table, the bottle of alcohol nearby. She listened to the drunken hoots and hollers that drifted in from down the hall. They were the sounds of other men like him. They would take her for themselves without a second thought, and there she was, ready to save them in court and throw another woman under the bus.

There was no way she was going to make it home. She'd find her death in the gun's barrel and she'd suffer through that same disgusting experience she suffered through all those years ago. Those late nights working hard to forget the pain, and all it did was bring her back full circle, right into the clutches of her most feared nightmare. His beady eyes stared at her, a small shimmer in the light of the dim room reflected off them.

"At least you didn't get fat," he said with a snicker. "I hate it when I date a girl and they get fat. Usually in their mid-twenties or something, they turn into a fucking cow. Then, I'm out with the boys and run into them and have to explain that she wasn't all that fat back when we dated. Gotta find a picture of them from before, but their social media is all fat pictures now, and I deleted everything with them the moment we split. It sucks."

"I'm not her," Cleopatra said.

"I'm sorry?"

"I'm not her. I'm not that girl. You killed her that day and that little girl didn't exist the second you wrapped your clammy little hands around her mouth and whispered for her not to scream. You killed her."

"Don't be so dramatic."

She didn't need to be dramatic; she needed to be strong. Men like him were pathetic. A dime a dozen. She dealt with assholes like him throughout her career.

They were stepping stones for her success. The richest CEOs of large companies around the world had hit her on left and right. She remained strong and fearless in every scenario. The only difference now is that this man had a gun. Despite what he did to her, he was as fragile as every other asshole with an overwhelming ego. Her father thought she was weak, but he didn't realize how strong she might become, not because of what happened, but despite it.

Men like Davis were nothing special. She needed to turn off the part of her that let him have power. She needed to believe her own words. That little girl died that day. Yes. He killed her. But from the ashes of that little girl, something else emerged—a monster to be reckoned with.

"You spent your entire life trying to find me," she said.

"That's right."

"I spent the same time trying to get away from you."

"I stayed with you."

"You haunted me."

"Is that a bad thing?"

She pulled the papers from the envelope and threw them into the air. They flew up and fluttered down like a slow rainfall. As he looked up, she reached for the gun. She was fast, but he was faster. She pressed her fingers against the cold steel of it, only to have it pulled away at the last second. Without missing a step, she reached up with her other hand and swung down. He yelped and dropped the gun as the letter opener went through his forearm. The gun tumbled to the floor, and she kicked it away, out of his reach. In another swift move, as the last of the papers flitted to the ground, she yanked the letter opener from his arm and stabbed him in the gut again and again.

Her mind swept over a memory from when she tried her hand at being a public defender. Her client had shanked a guy in the showers with a prison-made shiv. When he described it to her, he mentioned it had to be a flurry attack. Stab again and again so he didn't know which spot to defend, what was most painful, and that way when he gets to the infirmary, he's so full of holes that he goes down like a ship and never sets sail again.

That's what she did. She poked him so full of holes that he would never sail again. With wild swings, he shoved, pulled, and hit her until he finally landed a strike, causing her to sprawl across the desk and tumble to the floor. He leaped over the desk, but she rolled away, still clutching the letter opener and holding it up, ready to go again. He leaned against his desk. She waited near the door. The gun lay on the floor in the center of the office.

"If you run…" he said, gasping for air and attempting to hold his wounds. "I'll grab that gun and hunt you down… you'll be dead before you make the lobby. I can call out for them. They'll charge in here and do whatever I tell them to do."

"If you reach for that gun," she said, massaging her jaw where he struck her. "I'll stick this in your eye before you lay a finger on it."

"Stalemate."

"Not from where I'm standing."

"How do you figure?"

"You're poked full of holes. I only have a bruised jaw."

"I'm a man."

"I'm a woman."

"I'm bigger than you, stronger than you."

"You're weaker than me and bleeding like a cut brake line. Take a seat."

He looked at the chair where she had been sitting a few moments before. He plopped down into it.

"I take it you won't file these papers?"

"You already signed them. Drop them off yourself if you make it out of here alive."

"So, what? You're going to kill me?"

"You're the one who introduced the gun. Who keeps a gun in their office, anyway?"

He nodded and sucked his teeth. The question rattled around in his head as he inspected his wounds. He found one that seemed to bleed more than the others and stuck his finger into it with a groan.

"Like the little Dutch boy trying to save his town," Cleopatra said.

"Fuck you. I've had worse."

"What, those STDs rotting your dick?"

"You want to find out for yourself?"

"I'll cut it off if you even try."

"So, what do we do now? You gonna kill me? Call the cops?"

"Not sure."

"You know, if that gun goes off, six very drunk, very loyal men will run in here."

"I know. That's why I have the letter opener."

He laughed and pointed to his head to show that she was a thinker. He let out a deep groan and adjusted in his seat. She pulled one of the extra chairs from by the door and took a seat herself. They stared at each other across the room, eyeing the gun and then looking off as if they weren't plotting for a way to survive the night at the mercy of their tormentors.

"Why do you have a gun in your office?" Cleopatra asked again.

"Protection."

"From what?"

"Women I raped."

"You mean 'girls' you raped?"

He ignored this and stared at the gun, evaluating the extent of his injuries.

"It is you."

"We covered that."

"No, I mean, it is you. See, I thought for some time that I was chasing the high. Grabbing a young girl, a virgin. Shoving her, dominating her, making her mine and mine alone. I knew she would remember me forever. Even if I died the next day, that assault would be on her mind forever. I would have this unfettered power over a stranger, and yet, it was me who was at her mercy all this time. Your mercy. See, I tried it again. I tried it many times, but it was never the same. It was never as good as it was with you. We were both victims of each other."

"No. We're both victims of you, of your actions."

"You're right." He held up his hands in mock surrender. "So, what happens now? How do we end the stalemate? Which one of us wins?"

"Neither of us wins," Cleopatra said. "But, in every unpleasant situation, there is some good."

"Sending me to jail? That's the good I'm assuming?"

"Which would you prefer, death or jail?"

He stared at her, trying his best to read her, but getting nothing. All his power moves and corporate bravado offered nothing for the negotiation of life or death with his victim. Rather than answering, he left the question alone and stared at the gun, willing it into his hand.

He tried to urge his body to move, prepare it to leap across the room, snatch up the gun, and put an end to everything. His body didn't want to listen. Blood pooled around him and stuck him in his chair like glue.

"I can't believe it," she said. "You're trying to get the gun, aren't you?"

Again, he ignored her question. He had nothing left to say. Besides, the room was getting darker. Her words were too slow and he couldn't get his mouth to move and say the things he wanted it to. His head drooped. Still, he didn't lose sight of it, stared, hoping to see his own hands clutched around the butt, finger on the trigger, and Cleopatra's head at the other end of the barrel. With her death, his empire would be safe. With his death, the world would crumble.

As he stared, he saw a hand do exactly as he willed his own, only the hand wasn't his. The delicate fingers wrapped around it were slender with nails painted red and at the end of the barrel was his head. His eyelids drooped and the image of Cleopatra blurred into the vision of her he held in his head for so long. She was young and smiling, wandering off in search of a bathroom.

He heard her fumble around with something. A sharp pain in his leg brought him back to the moment. He looked down at the letter opener sticking up from his leg. His mouth opened in a scream as his voice rang out. Her hand closed over it and emptied a handful of thumbtacks into his mouth. As he screamed and struggled, they ran down his throat and poked little holes in it. He flailed and fell out of the chair and onto the floor. He coughed and spat out a few tacks, but the others worked their way further into his throat. His eyes dropped again and eventually, he stopped moving. She checked for a pulse but found none. To be sure, she stuck the letter opener into him a few times, but he didn't flinch.

Cleopatra stood alone in the room. Her heart raced, beating out of her chest as she stood over her tormentor's corpse. She closed her eyes and counted aloud as she took deep breaths and let out a slow exhale. Her trembling hands stiffened and went steady. She adjusted her clothes, and checked her reflection in a mirror by the wet bar. Sprays of blood painted her blouse and face. She did her best to wipe off what she could with a melted ice cube. Then she made her way out to the conference rooms. She whispered into their ears.

They told their guests to head home for the night and that everything was fine.

"Just some papers to sign," one of them said.

Once their guests were gone, they made their way into the office, where a lone figure lay sprawled out across the floor.

"Have a little too much to drink, boss?" Bill asked.

Bill slipped on a sheet of paper as he approached his dead friend. He leaned down and picked it up and saw that it was the signed pages of their settled lawsuit. As he held it up to show to the others, a flash of light and a loud bang went off. Red sprayed across the paper. They looked from one to another, trying to make sense of everything until their eyes wandered over to Cleopatra and the gun in her hand, raised and aimed at them. Then the knuckle on her index finger turned white and, with a flash of light, everything went dark. More shots followed and screams accompanied all the shots until both went silent and the only sound was the click-clack of a pair of heels leaving the office.

| 23 |

GUILT

The corpse walked, sinewy muscles and torn tendons rippling with each step. It turned to where I hid, its wide-eyes and fleshless skull glaring at me, knowing what I did.

| 24 |

PEANUT BUTTER AND JELLY

I should know better than to transport your dead body in a rolled-up carpet, but I'm stubborn and no one's here to stop me. It's much harder than it looks to pull you out of the back of an SUV when I'm 5'6 and 120 pounds.

The last girl slipped out of my hands. The carpet unraveled, and she flopped out onto the open road. It took me all day to wrap her up again and drag her into the woods. She was as stubborn in death as she was in life.

I back the SUV into the edge of the woods. You plop into the dirt. Nowhere to roll. I grip the carpet's frayed edge and our journey begins. Somewhere in these woods, there's a nice little spot where I can dig a tidy little hole for you.

Maybe for once, I'll do something right. Then again, I can't do anything right. That's all I ever hear.

"Get a better job. Get a raise. Clean this. Do that."

Shut up, mom.

So I find comfort elsewhere. With people like you. You listen to me and let me talk and say what I need to say. There's no judgment or criticism. Only silence. I love you even though you're dead. I'll bury you in a delightful spot where you can see the sky.

Well, you won't be able to see the sky, because you'll be under a few feet of dirt. Might have to cut you up into tiny pieces too, depending on how much of a hole I can dig. And you're dead, don't forget that. You won't be seeing much, but it's the thought that counts. Right?

Yes, I said pieces. That's why I wear this backpack filled with heavy tools. There might be some dismemberment in your near future. Think about it—if I cut you into pieces, dig a deep hole, and stack them, you'll take up less space, making it harder for anyone to find you. If you're spread out, someone would have more of a chance of finding a piece of you. That might lead them to the rest of you. In twenty years, with the way this area is developing, it'll all be condos anyway. They'll either dig you up or pave you over, but by then, I'll be long gone, dead, or already in jail at the rate I'm going.

The newspapers call me the Sunnyvale Slayer. I don't like it. The only reason the name stuck is that they hadn't linked me to those other disappearances. Plus alliteration. I love alliteration. I don't think I could spell it to save my life, though.

I've killed more in Milpitas than Sunnyvale. Milpitas Monster would be great, but it's the name of an old monster flick shot there in the 80s and I might get sued. I've also considered the Bay Area Butcher, Santa Clara County Killer. Any of those would be fine.

Until the newspaper links my crimes, I'm Sunnyvale Slayer. I guess the name isn't so bad, but it's the definitive nature of it that bothers me. Trapping my crimes to one locale diminishes the hard work I've done.

I'm not the only killer on the loose. It's like Santa Cruz in the 70s over here. The Campbell Killer. Nice name. Straight to the point. The K sounds make it more brutal. I wonder if he likes his name. Or her name. I don't think I'm in a place to make assumptions. I mean, no one would expect the Sunnyvale Slayer to be a scrawny Asian dude. Especially because all my victims are Black.

The papers and profilers who have launched blogs about me say that I'm a middle-aged male, possibly Black or Latino and athletically built with a steady home life but disappear for hours at a time using work as a cover. These shrinks are so far up their own asses trying not to offend anyone these days. I'm the total stereotype aside from being Asian. I live with my sadistic, neurotic mother. My dad was an asshole too, but he had the courtesy of dying when I was young. And I don't have a job. I don't even lie about having a job. I just leave when I need to leave because who gives a shit about me or where I'm going?

As I drag you deeper into the woods, my arms burn and my back goes numb. Sweat pours down from my hair, and I can feel the wetness on my back. I push through. I should have brought water or at least a snack. Maybe a peanut butter and jelly sandwich. Peanut butter and jelly is the greatest food ever to exist in this world. It's so perfect and delicious. With the right toaster, the sky's the limit. Fluffernutter is good too, or honey and peanut butter. Anything with peanut butter, really. I once had a hamburger with peanut butter and it was incredible. It was called the Elvis Burger. He liked peanut butter a lot too I guess. I've never been a fan. Hopefully, this isn't me following in his footsteps.

Not really a fan of dying in the bathroom on the toilet. But then, what is a good way to die? Certainly not the way I killed you. That was more brutal than I meant for it to be when I started. I'll probably have a peaceful death under the careful watch of your family members, a lawyer, my bitch mother telling me she told me so, and an executioner.

What was I talking about?

Oh! Peanut butter and jelly. No! Right, burying you. I should pay more attention. I really want peanut butter and jelly right now. Did you know that the invention of peanut butter is often wrongfully attributed to George Washington Carver? Just to clarify, I'm not telling you this because you're Black. I'm not one of those guys that tells every Black person he meets he voted for Obama. I mean, I was twelve during his election, but you know what I mean. Anyway, George Washington Carver had 325 uses for peanuts, but none of them were peanut butter! To have been his assistant... A boy can dream, right?

The Aztecs had a peanut butter paste a long time ago. The peanut butter we eat now, with jelly, was actually invented by John Harvey Kellogg. Kellogg as in the cereal family. It's an ironic twist, isn't it? Cereal and serial killers, a play on words that's as unsettling as it is amusing. I'd choose peanut butter and jelly as my last meal. Obviously. An entire stack of them with white bread and milk.

I wonder if other killers liked their names. BTK picked his name in a letter to the newspaper. Zodiac too. Son of Sam picked his, but he hated it later on. Found God and all that crap. The Axeman of New Orleans got to pick his name. Now that is one hell of a name. What could I do like that? Slasher of Sunnyvale? Monster of Milpitas? Butcher of the Bay. Wow, that has a magnificent ring to it. I wonder if I can claim that name in the papers? Do papers even print this stuff anymore? Or would it be too triggering for the current generation of news-hungry hipsters? True crime is all the rage. No one cares about the victims. If it bleeds, it leads.

I stumble to a halt and collapse onto the ground. Leaves crunch beneath me like chomping on chunky peanut butter. This spot seems as good as any. Far enough away from the road, but not so deep into the woods in case I visit. You're my closest friend, the only one who's seen me at my worst. My most vulnerable. Well, not including the others, but there was something special about you. I really liked you. I don't know what it is. Was... I don't know what it was. Or maybe I loved you because of the last words you said to me, "my baby... who will watch my baby? Who will raise him? Please..."

Those words echo through my mind. The tears on your face, your quivering lip as I strangled you. Your son, Ethan, you said his name when I started chasing you. I bet you made a lot of peanut butter and jelly for him. I'll try to find him when we're done here. Maybe I can make him a peanut butter and jelly sandwich too. He can come here and see you. I can let him climb into your hole and spend eternity with you if you'd like. That would be nice. You seemed so worried about him.

When I was a kid, school always gave away free peanut butter and jelly sandwiches if you didn't have lunch. After moving out to California and looking back, it was a strange way to go about doing things. Every morning, one of the faculty members from the principal's office would go to each classroom and take our order for lunch. Depending on what we picked, they would give a certain color poker chip. At lunch, you'd show them the chip, collect your food, then pay at the end of the line. If you lost your chip or didn't have money, you'd get peanut butter and jelly by default. Nowadays, they wouldn't dare do such a thing with kids and peanut allergies and whatnot. But back then, I would line up to give my order in the morning and they would look at me like I was some sort of freak when I ordered the free peanut butter and jelly. They would tell me not to bother ordering it because they can hand it to me at lunch with no issue. I couldn't take the risk. I needed to make sure they had one for me, so I kept lining up and putting in my order for a peanut butter and jelly sandwich. To be honest, they were probably the worst ones I ever had. They gobbed on the pastes with no thought of dispersing them. But I kept coming back and getting them.

I think it all goes back to the day I was born. When my mom went into labor, the hospital was going through a strike. They had no kitchen staff and so the only food she could eat during labor was a peanut butter and jelly sand-wich.

Growing up, whenever I spent time with friends, I always asked for peanut butter and jelly. I think I assumed it was free because it was always free at school, and at the hospital from the stories my mom told me, and therefore the easiest choice for my lunch. When I got older, I realized it was probably more of a pain to accommodate me. My friends' parents would say, "look what we got just for you!" There I would be, chewing on peanut butter and jelly, while everyone else ate ham and cheese.

I don't think I ever had a chance at being normal. Since the day I was born, peanut butter and jelly have ruled my life.

After catching my breath and sucking in the crisp fall air, I cut the tape and unravel you. You roll out and jiggle to a halt. Your beautiful eyes stare up at the sky and we lay here watching the clouds roll by. Calm. Quiet. Relaxing.

As I dismember you, I tell you everything I can't tell anyone else. You listen as I slice off your ears. You watch the sky through your plucked out eyes and don't say a word as I cut out your tongue.

I break down as I confess my loneliness. You don't judge me. Not like the others. No one understands me but you. I tell you of my mother and show you the scars she left me. One that covered my back. Boiling water when she caught me in the shower. I remove your lower leg and show you the scar on my knee. My mom was driving, and I sat in the back. I made a joke to a friend, and she didn't like it. She reached back and dug her nails into my leg. It was the only part of me she could reach. I screeched for her to stop. The pain was too much for the little six-year-old me. My friend cried and covered his eyes. My mom dug her nails in until she felt blood on her fingertips, then she twisted. The scars are there, you can count them and see the indent of each nail. The scars on my wrists are mine, though. You don't judge me for those. I cut off your hand and brush your fingers along the raised skin, then I kiss the back of your hand and roll over, holding it in my arms like a stuffed animal.

A calm breeze rattles the leaves on the trees around us like a soothing white noise. The sun drops, and the day turns nice and cool. The scent of iron, wet blood on the dry leaves, mingles in the air with the smell of the approaching autumn. Time gets away and I doze off, our limbs intertwined.

I awaken to the sound of rustling. I rub my eyes and stretch and look at you, still staring up at the sky. Not going anywhere. Still sleeping.

Then I jolt up. I remember I'm in the woods, lying next to you. The rustling noise continues, and I duck back down. I flip onto my stomach and scan the horizon.

Wild animals? Hiker? Police? A wild animal police hiker? What could it be?

A few feet away from our spot, there's a dip in the ground I can't see. A small cliff about my height. I crawl to the edge and peek over.

There could be a dozen cops, lights flashing and guns pointed. I picture my mother among them, finger wagging and a belt at the ready to beat me for making her look bad.

Instead, what I see is a thing of beauty. A crust-cut-off-chunky-peanut-butter-and-jelly type of beauty.

A man, covered in dirt, sitting on the edge of a large hole, eating. Beside him lay the naked body of a dead woman. He swings his legs and bounces around as he inspects the food he's eating, enjoying every bite. I hide and watch for a moment, focusing on the food in his hand. Is it? Despite the strong smell of autumn in the surrounding leaves, and the stench of dismembered corpses, the sweet aroma of peanut butter wafts over to me, and I know I've met someone special, someone like me.

It's a peanut butter and jelly sandwich.

I can't believe my eyes. Someone like me, finding the same spot in the same woods and taking his own friend there to say goodbye. My cheeks tighten as a smile creeps across my face for the first time in a long time.

I raise my hands, stand up and whisper.

"Hello?"

He jumps. His eyes, big and wide. He doesn't get up or run away. Instead, he freezes and stares at me through thick glasses, still eating.

"Relax," I say. I step closer, hands still in the air. "I want to show you something. You're not in trouble, I promise. In fact, quite the opposite."

I disappear for a moment, then run back over to the tiny cliff. He's standing now, holding his shovel, his knuckles white from his tight grip. I wave at him with your severed hand, holding it by the forearm.

"Hello!" I call out.

His white knuckles loosen on the shovel, and it falls to the ground.

"Nice to meet you," I say, extending your hand for a shake. "I'm the Butcher of the Bay."

He pauses. Confused.

I sigh, "Sunnyvale Slayer."

With those words, his eyes light up. A smile spreads across his face and I see all the teeth in his mouth. Pieces of soft white bread stick between his teeth.

"I'm the Campbell Killer," he says.

It looks like time to bid you farewell. I'll get your hole nice and deep and leave the pieces of you in there for no one to find. If I can find your son, I'll bring him to you soon and you can be together forever. I'll never forget you, but it seems I've made a new friend. A perfect friend.

The jelly to my peanut butter.

| 25 |

RANSOM

I said, "The ransom money was dropped off by her dad."

"Oh, I thought you said, 'No ransom money? Chop off her head.'"

| 26 |

THE LAST DEPARTURE

Earth, central to all life and innovation, gasped its last breaths under the weight of humanity's folly. From the towering metropolises to the quiet countrysides, the countdown had begun. For years, scientists and visionaries whispered of an escape, a sanctuary among the stars — a new beginning on Mars.

Screams of discontent echoed through the crowd that protested outside the fortified launch complex.

"Let us in," someone screamed.

"Cowards," another shouted.

"Unworthy," many chanted.

A single entry gate stood between them and their salvation — those majestic ships, sleek and elegant, the last salvation for the best of humanity. Carter pushed his way to the front, holding up his work badge. He was on time, early even, and yet by the looks of things, he was too late.

"I'm an ElysieM employee," he shouted over the crowd. A guard, standing strong at the entrance, looked him in the eye, then looked away, scanning the crowd once again. "Did you hear me?"

Carter shoved his way forward. Hands grabbed and pulled him in all directions.

"There's a line," someone yelled.

"Where do you think you're going? You one of them?" Another shouted as they struck him.

Carter flinched but continued his efforts, shoving forward, pushing people away. When he finally made it to the gate, he held up his badge once again.

"I'm an employee," he said. "I'm guaranteed a seat."

"Everyone is already on board. No more room," the guard said.

"No, there must be a mistake. I work there. I was told to report."

"It's too late," the guard said. "Everyone is already inside. Get lost."

"What do you mean?"

A hand grabbed Carter's shoulder and spun him around. Carter was ready to fight when he recognized the familiar face of a friend, Vince. They worked together in accounting and spent the better part of the last five years managing the budget for Project Exodus. Without them, the entire project would have fallen apart.

"They fucked us," Vince said.

"What do you mean?"

"We're not worthy. They lied to half the company and gave the wrong times. Only higher-ups are on board, and mechanics, a few pilots. But everyone else got fucked. Everyone from IR3 and down."

"Are you kidding me?"

"We're unworthy," Vince said. "They fucked us."

Carter heard the pain seeping through Vince's voice. Vince had a wife and kids. He loved them more than anything. The only reason he took the job was to secure them a spot on the Mars colony.

"Shit, Vince," Carter said. "I'm so sorry. Your family?"

"They're over there."

He led Carter through the crowd.

ElysieM, the company behind the most ambitious government project in history, initially disguised their selection process as a lottery. But once ElysieM announced the first few thousand "winners," people realized the truth. The chosen were the elite: the wealthy, billionaires, and tech giants. Among them were geniuses and scientists, selections that most people accepted. But there were also the unskilled children of the rich, influencers, mistresses, celebrities, and members of the clergy — with some religions notably underrepresented. Public outrage followed, with a few winners even being murdered by angry mobs. As a response, they kept the identities of future selections secret. However, when the last list of chosen ones leaked, it became clear that most of humanity never had a chance.

That's when the riots began.

The eruption of violence spread across the world like a ferocious hurricane encroaching on a small town. An unfamiliar energy charged the atmosphere. Tension grew so thick, it became impossible to breathe without admitting there was a storm coming. What began as murmurs of discontent erupted into a cacophony of anger. Protestors, rioters, looters, flooded into the streets, faces contorted with anger and each breath, a scream into the building storm.

The crowd surged, waving makeshift banners and crude signs above their heads. They called themselves The Unworthy, adopting the name as a rallying cry for their movement to demand a new lottery.

Businesses shuttered their doors and boarded up their windows, but it was futile. The crowd looted and set ablaze anything tied to ElysieM or owned by one of the fat cats named as a Future Survivor.

The end was nigh, and a single person became the lone decider of who lives and who dies. Government forces fought back and pushed hard. The storm made landfall. The sounds of gunfire and tear gas canisters being launched through the air replaced chants and prayers.

Carter and Vince weren't the type to protest. They never took to the streets or voiced their concerns up the chain of command at ElysieM. They kept their heads down, crunched the numbers and made it work so they could secure a seat for themselves. Vince wanted to protect his family. Carter wasn't sure what he wanted, but he knew that whatever he wanted, he wasn't finding on Earth.

Vince pointed over to a makeshift tent erected of tarps and pallets.

"They're over there," he said. "Just don't say anything about what happened."

"They don't know?"

"Do you know how hard it is to tell your wife and kids, your two-year-old daughter, that the world is ending and we're all going to die?" Vince grabbed Carter's collar and pulled his face close to his own. His words came out as a growl. "She doesn't even understand death. Everything I worked for, all those family dinners I missed, working my ass off to get us a place aboard that ugly ass ship. And all for nothing. We're all fucked."

"I'm not the bad guy here, Vince," Carter said. He removed Vince's grasp from his collar and patted his shoulder.

"I know, Carter. It's all so messed up. I feel like such an idiot. I should've sabotaged everything, prevented anyone from boarding, and ensured that these things never got built. Screw everyone... Just tell my family we're waiting for our turn."

Carter nodded and followed Vince. Inside, the kids were tired, sprawled out and sleeping on makeshift beds fashioned of sleeping bags and an old mattress. Their home was one of many to be destroyed in the wake of protests. More hackers exposed behind-the-scenes information, including a list of employees who worked on Project Exodus. Carter was lucky. When the protestors arrived, he stayed at a neighbor's. They didn't mind. It was an old couple he had befriended and helped with groceries and technology over the years. They had no hope, no desire to leave the world. Carter listened through the wall as the looters destroyed the life he built.

"Hey, Martha," Carter whispered, hugging Vince's wife, careful not to wake the kids.

Their makeshift camp had a musty odor and dinginess to it. A heaviness built in his chest as he looked around at Vince's family, knowing the truth unfolding outside.

"Hey, nice to see you," Martha said. "Any news?"

"Nothing yet, they're still waiting for clearance," Vince said. He couldn't look his wife in the eyes as he said it.

"What's taking them so long?" She asked.

"Not sure," Carter said. "Were you guys able to grab what you needed?"

"Not really," Martha said. "They came fast. Broke down the door, we barely escaped. Thankfully, we packed for the flight, so we grabbed that stuff. You're welcome to anything you'd like."

She gestured over to a backpack. Carter could see inside that there were a few cans of meat and some crackers, but not much else. He set down his backpack and pulled out a freezer bag filled with flash frozen meals ready to eat.

"Here. I got these from my neighbor. Do you have any water?"

"Oh, no, we couldn't. That's yours," Vince said.

"No, really. I have more. It's fine. You know, my great grandfather was a hostage during the early wars. He was a kid when it happened. They marched him across the island. He had to let his baby brother sleep on his chest during the night so he didn't get sick from the cold mud during the rainy season. My grandpa lived to be 90, but he still shopped at the boys' department because he was so malnourished in those camps as a kid. Really, take this bag. I have more. I want the kids to eat."

"Thank you, really, thank you," Martha said.

She took the meals to the corner and filled them with water. Soon enough, the smell of food filled their tent, and the kids stirred from their sleep, hungry and curious. They shared all they could. It was salty and disgusting, but in a way, it was one of the greatest meals Carter had ever tasted. Looking around at all the faces of his friend's children and his wonderful wife, he knew he missed out on something in his own life. It wasn't for lack of trying, it wasn't in the cards for him.

That's when the commotion started. Screams and shouts from outside shattered their moment of peace.

"Stay here, but get ready," Vince said to Martha. She nodded and started packing the few items they had. The kids knew the drill. Since the scientists came out and told everyone the world was ending, it had been a bitter fight from one day to the next. Vince didn't need to tell them twice.

Carter stood outside, Vince joined him, finishing the last of his meal. Steam rose in the day's cold. He ate the last bite, then tossed his trash into the street. There was no point in pretending a trash can mattered anymore. The planet was already dead.

They looked on in horror as the crowd pushed forward. They spilled through the gates and out onto the tarmac. People rushed toward the ships as the second and third layers of security opened fire at the stampede of desperate people. The sounds of bullets smacking into the flesh were louder than Carter expected. Dead bodies collapsed and the crowd behind them crushed their bodies underfoot as they overtook the guards.

Martha stepped out and joined them. The kids were still inside, as instructed.

"What's happening?" she asked.

Vince looked at her, then at the crowd and over at the ships. She stopped him and said what she knew deep inside before he had the chance to come up with another excuse.

"We were never getting on, were we?"

"I tried so hard, so hard. I really thought we had a chance."

"Vince, you did your best. There's nothing to be sorry about. I had a feeling. You know you could have told me."

"I'm sorry. I thought there might be some way, that maybe it was all..."

"It's alright. I understand. At least we're here together. You too, Carter?"

Carter nodded. "In the words of a wise man, 'they fucked us.'"

Vince nodded and shook his head as the violence worsened with every whistle, every scream, every gunshot. People climbed walls, then fell at the crack of a rifle. Further down the tarmac, the "lottery" winners hurried onto the ships.

Vince's family came out and joined them as they watched. Martha could have shielded their eyes, and she was about to, but with a shrug of her shoulders, she seemed to admit that nothing mattered anymore. Carter and Vince's family climbed onto a toppled building and watched from a better view.

"Mom, what's happening? I thought we were going there."

"It's okay. Just hug your brother."

Time passed, an instant and an eternity all at once. Finally, an announcement sounded across the tarmac.

"Today is the day. We are sorry we could not take all humanity with us, but rest assured, we are doing our best to continue the legacy of the human race among the stars. Your sacrifices today are not in vain. It is because you all have chosen so bravely to let life continue on without you. Your memories will all live on as humanity colonizes the stars and beyond. As humanity continues to prosper and drive beyond the known universe, your memories will all be with us. Thank you and goodbye. Goodbye all, goodbye Earth. May God watch over us all."

As if the crowd wasn't already a roar, it roared even louder. The anguish of the collective human race shook the world beneath their feet, which blended into the thunder of the engines, which, too, shook the ground.

The ships lifted off the ground. A dozen altogether. The angry mob couldn't help but stare in awe. Even if they hated the ship and everything the project became, no one could deny the beauty of the vessels as they drifted up and ascended through the atmosphere. The last ship sputtered. It rose off the ground, then fell back, the engines kicking on, then turning off.

It taxied down the runway, engines kicking on at last and holding steady as it moved, hovering a few inches off the ground. Desperate members of the crowd threw themselves at the ship's landing gear, and at the sides of the ship where they climbed, trying to find any handhold or foothold to secure a place. Their hands grasped metal, feet scraped against the ship's surface. The ship lifted off, flying down the runway, those desperate souls holding on for their dear life, only to lose their grips. They tumbled down to the Earth, desperation ending in tragedy as their bodies smacked against the tarmac and the ship joined the others in the sky.

Vince wrapped his arm around his kids and threw an arm over Carter as well. The unworthy ones left behind to die watched as the ship turned away from them and aimed up into the stars. Anger melted away and gave way to helplessness. Hopelessness.

"There goes the supposed best of humanity," Vince whispered so only Carter could hear.

The engines roared once more as the ships shot across the sky, then looped back overhead as if taunting those left behind. But as the fleeting peace seemed to settle, an explosion shattered the calm. Flames erupted from the first spacecraft, tearing through it like a hammer smashing glass, scattering debris in all directions. One by one, the other ships followed, bursting into flames and breaking apart, their fiery trails streaking across the sky. The last ship, which had struggled to take off, continued its flight path, soaring further than the rest.

The crowd watched with bated breath, their initial anger giving way to shock and a flicker of hope as the plane flew on. But that hope was short-lived. The final spaceship, too, erupted in a fireball and plummeted to the Earth below.

The unworthy ran for cover, evading the falling shrapnel and diving out of harm's way. As the ships took off, their cries were a mixture of rage and frustration, directed at each other in their shared despair. But when the ships exploded, their screams shifted to a piercing blend of fear and anguish. Now uncertainty gripped them, causing their voices to rise in a haunting chorus of terror as they faced the unknown and grappled with their helplessness. Their unworthiness.

Vince and his family also leapt to their feet, mouths wide open in horrified shock, their hands grasped over them.

Carter stayed seated and smiled. He couldn't have foreseen such a tragedy, but in that moment, he couldn't help but smile. It was over. The supposed best of the best that humanity offered was all dead. The Earth would soon follow and with that last glimmer of hope, they were all doomed. Not a soul would survive. Perhaps those on board still had the best outcome, a quick, painless death. Maybe that was the plan all along, or maybe it was a lucky coincidence. Either way, Carter dusted himself off and whistled a tune as he bid Vince's family farewell and headed back to his apartment to wait out the end of the world.

| 27 |

TRICK

There was a bowl left outside with a sign that hung overhead which read, "please, take only one." Billy laughed and dumped the bowl into his backpack, unaware of the importance of the sign and the creature he had awoken.

Up next is a bonus story that intertwines with the events of my first novel, *Coffee Rings*

Enjoy this taste of the horrors from
Kato M. M. Guzman and Slingstone Media
Available now!

| 28 |

COFFEE AFTER MIDNIGHT

A *Coffee Rings* Short Story

The bright sign flickered through the fog. It promised warmth and shelter, and a hearty meal. With it came a feeling of unease that will haunt any patron whenever they think back to their visit.

For normal people, anyway. The ones living in ignorance of the darkness surrounding them.

Others are creatures, monsters in human flesh, unimaginable things that go bump in the night. For them, Coffee Rings is a light in the dark, and they are all moths. The light draws them in, for better or worse.

For the locals, rumors swirl about that diner. They swap stories around campfires and in the darkness of a sleepover. They say things about that little diner that may or may not be true. The outlandish tales are traded like cards with a dealer in a dusty casino. One wrong hand, one failed bluff, and the end could be as looming as the nearest shadow.

Coffee Rings wasn't only a diner, it was a piece of the town. It lived and breathed like any landmark, its walls drenched in secrets, the diner itself, weary of all who enter, and protective of those who keep it alive.

It was a time capsule of mid century architecture on the outside. The front of the diner had thick neon lights running around a bright theater-style marquee which boasted specials. Metallic lining clung to the outer walls. A renovation tore down a third of the building and rebuilt it in the cocaine-inspired style of the late 80s. What remained was a mismatched diner, frozen in two very different decades. No matter its faults, it was the only place in town serving food throughout the night.

Truckers polished off the last of the pancake batter in the early morning hours. They long since moved along to bigger highways in bigger cities. The other workers went home with yawns and sore feet. A patron between three and five in the morning was a rarity in that town in the middle of the week. Gladys liked the calm, but dreaded it as much. She was more alone in those few hours than most people would ever be in their entire lives.

A lone cook who preferred to keep to himself tended the kitchen. He often took this time to clean the stove and take out the trash. That day, he had problems to deal with and needed rest, so he took a nap in his car, parked out back. He insisted Gladys could wake him up if anyone came by looking for a hot meal. She assured him she understood, but would only offer coffee until he rested enough to tend to the kitchen without burning himself.

She brewed a fresh pot of coffee and counted out the register. She stuffed the day's profits into an envelope and left enough change to start the day that had just begun.

The bell above the door chimed.

Gladys walked out into the main dining area where she found two large men waiting for her. They dressed in all black and wore ski masks. The man closest to Gladys pointed a shotgun at her. The other man locked the door and flipped the "Yes, we're open" sign to "Sorry, we're closed." He didn't have any weapons that she could see, but it wouldn't have mattered even if he did.

Gladys wasn't sure why she even kept the sign in the window, considering it was a 24/7 operation. Even on Christmas, throughout the holiday season, Coffee Rings never closed and Gladys never took a day off.

"Money," the man nearest Gladys said. "All of it. Now."

"This isn't the first time I've been through this, honey." Her voice stayed calm. She was more annoyed than nervous. She even rolled her eyes at the inconvenience of it all. "Safe is downstairs. Won't make any trouble."

The men followed, keeping the shotgun aimed at Gladys. She led them through the kitchen, where there was a door to an office. The robbers threw each other unsure looks as they looked around the small room.

"This is an office," the main robber said. "I thought you said it was downstairs."

Gladys pushed the wall. It moved back about an inch. Gladys slid the door to the side, revealing a staircase leading to darkness. The robbers peered down the staircase but couldn't see beyond a few steps. An icy breeze drifted up. They shivered and took a step forward.

"Alright," the second robber said. "Down the stairs. Let's go."

"Is there a light?" The main robber asked.

"There is," Gladys said. "It's on one of those pull chain things, but it's down at the bottom. Is that going to be a problem, big fella?"

"Alright, then. Go first." The robber motioned with the shotgun.

They followed Gladys down the steps and into the darkness. They expected their eyes to adjust, but it was so dark they couldn't even see their noses. Their feet hit the soft dirt of the basement floor. Darkness encompassed them, and the stale air swirled around and embraced them. They spun around, ready to make a break for it but they couldn't even see the light at the top of the stairs.

"Turn on the light," the main robber shouted. His voice gave away his fear. The darkness felt vast.

Cold.

Empty.

A light clicked on. The soft glow of a dim yellow bulb illuminated a few feet around it. The walls were old stones, stacked tall. Gladys dragged her hand along a part of the stone wall. Her eyes pulled back in a smile, her crow's feet scrunched and her gray hair fell around her shoulders. The robbers didn't notice the shift in her appearance. They weren't meant to.

"Where's the safe, lady?" One of them asked.

"These stones have been here for ages," she said, ignoring them. "The stones themselves are old as time, but them serving as the foundation for this building? Many centuries ago, there lived an old woman who stacked these rocks and built the home that once stood here."

"We're here for money, not a history lesson."

"You're here for much more than you think," Gladys continued to caress the wall, ignoring the men. "The woman who stacked these rocks embedded a power into them. Magic. Sorcery. Something good to some, evil to others. Look closer, now. You'll see the letters and the symbols form."

The robbers rolled their eyes but, as their vision finally adjusted to the dark; they noticed symbols etched into each of the stones. They couldn't help but reach out and touch them. The stones were gelid to the touch. The robber pulled his hand back and inspected it for frostbite.

"A few hundred years locked up in an old building with nowhere to go isn't pleasant for anyone," Gladys continued. "No matter the skills at your fingertips."

Gladys turned toward the robbers. In the yellow light, her true nature showed. They saw her rotted face and the skeleton beneath, with decayed chunks of flesh hanging off her bones. An insect crawled from one hole in her head into another. Her waitress uniform was dusty and tattered, smeared with blood. She reached up to her cheek and pinched a piece of her skin and pulled until it tore from the rest of her face. She held it out for the robbers to take. Maggots crawled in and out of that piece of flesh. A wretched odor drifted up to their noses.

The one with the shotgun puked and stumbled back, desperate to get away from Gladys. He tripped over something. The shotgun fell out of his hands and slid away into the darkness. He fumbled for his phone in his pocket. When he finally turned on the flashlight, he saw what he tripped over. The empty eye sockets and tattered remnants of an old ski mask on a smiling skeleton stared back at him. He got to his feet and faced back to the light, only to find himself alone. From somewhere in the darkness, he heard his friend scream, until it ended with a gurgle and the sound of a thump. Then silence.

"Frankie?"

The warm grip of a hand landed on his shoulder. He sighed with relief until he looked down and saw the decayed flesh of the hand and the maggots wriggling around in the skin. Gladys stepped back into the light. She reached up to his face and held his cheeks like a man doting on his dog.

"Please, I'm sorry. I'm so sorry. I needed the money. I won't ever do this again."

Gladys smiled and dug her hands into his face and pulled off his cheeks. His feet wouldn't move. His body froze. Gladys tore him apart, piece by piece, without saying a word, pulling a long sliver of flesh from his face that pulled down his neck until it finally released from his body and dangled in her hand.

"I told you I've been through this before, honey," Gladys said.

She reached up and pulled the chain that hung from the light sending the room into total darkness.

Moments later, Gladys walked into her office, closing the hidden door. She brushed off her clean waitress uniform. She was back to her normal self and ready to get back to work. She unlocked the front door and flipped the sign back to say, "Yes, we're open."

A breeze swept through the diner, tossing the napkins and sending them fluttering to the floor. Gladys knew what that meant. She turned back to the kitchen and found a bloody and scared girl standing before her. The girl gasped for breath, dressed in her uniform, covered in stab wounds and drenched in blood. Looking down at herself, she then gazed up at Gladys. She wanted to scream, but all she could do was cry. She wanted to speak, but words couldn't form. So she cried more. Gladys wrapped her arm around Elissa.

"Oh no, honey," Gladys said.

"Gladys?" Elissa asked. Tears streamed down her cheeks as her eyes darted around the diner. "How did I get here?"

Elissa stared at her bloody hands.

"Have a seat, honey."

Elissa sat down at the counter as she struggled to catch her breath. Gladys walked around and leaned on her elbows, staring into Elissa's scared eyes.

"Listen to me. Look at me, Elissa." Gladys was serious. Elissa turned to her, wide-eyed and confused. "Someone killed you, a man most likely. It's always a man."

"What do you mean?"

"What do you remember?"

Elissa's eyes fluttered across the countertop as she searched her memory.

"There was someone in my house. That creepy guy who keeps staring at me."

"That sounds right. When one of us gets killed, we end up back here."

"Killed?"

"Looks like it, honey."

"I have to work here forever now?" Elissa scrunched her nose, looking around the diner as if seeing for the first time.

"Well, it ain't that bad. Days come and go. You make the best out of it. You get to see the world change around you, but everything here will stay the same."

"What about my friends? My family?"

"You can see them, but they won't recognize you. It's an odd thing, like I said. They'll look you right in the eye and tell you their order, but they won't recognize you for all their worth. It'll kill you all over again when it happens. Best to let me serve anyone you know."

"This is forever?"

"Until you get forgotten. When everyone who loved you is dead, or they finally move on, you'll disappear. I've seen it happen a few times here and there. The limits of the heart would surprise you."

"How long have you been here?"

"Too long."

"How are you remembered?"

"I'm something else entirely, honey."

Gladys looked out the window as a car pulled in. "You can wash up in the back. Customers won't be too happy seeing you like this. I'll show you the ropes later. You're going to be as alright as you can be, baby girl."

Elissa walked to the back. She took quick steps as she processed everything. She tried not to look down at the blood.

Gladys greeted the customer and led him to a small booth in the corner. She offered him a kind smile. He glanced at the lipstick stain on her tooth as he sat down. He seemed the type to want to be alone, so she didn't bother with the small talk. His eyes were red with dark bags. His clothes were stale. The wrinkles on his face showed a lifetime of sorrow. Gladys knew the type. The diner seemed to attract them.

She put a menu in front of him.

"Welcome to Coffee Rings," Gladys said.

About the Author

Kato M. M. Guzman is an indigenous, mixed-race author proud of his Chamorro heritage. Originally from the small town of Glocester, Rhode Island, he now lives in San Jose, California. As a first-time author, Kato crafted this collection himself with a DIY spirit to bring his unique vision to life.

KatoMMGuzman.com